"It is clear that Yael loves children. Her compassion[...] those with differing abilities offers a roadmap for combining yoga and art in an inclusive environment. Drawing on scientific principles, well-documented resources, and her own experience, she empowers her reader with organizational tips, varied strategies, and easy-to-follow project ideas. This book will help you foster creativity, self-regulation techniques, and enthusiasm in your classroom, home, or clinic"

~ Louise Goldberg, author of Yoga Therapy for Children with Autism and Special Needs *and* Classroom Yoga Breaks-Brief Exercises to Create Calm

"Yael has given us more than a book—she's given us a gift. It's a thoughtful, compassionate, and deeply practical guide rooted in lived experience and evidence-based practice. As the founder of the Ed Asner Family Center for neurodivergent families and a mother of six, four of whom are autistic, I feel this book is a vital resource for anyone seeking to foster self-regulation, connection, and artistic expression for children with autism and other diverse learning needs.

What sets this guide apart is its clear, trauma-informed approach. Yael reminds us that safety is the foundation for learning and beautifully integrates science and soul to show how art and yoga can create the conditions for growth. With step-by-step scripts, easy-to-follow visuals, and powerful insights into the brain/body connection, this book doesn't just tell you why these practices work, it shows you how to make them work in real world settings.

Whether you're a teacher, therapist, caregiver, or parent, this book empowers you to build flexible, inclusive programs that center play, simplicity, and emotional safety. It's not just a curriculum—it's a roadmap to helping children thrive through creativity, movement, and mindful engagement."

~ Navah Paskowitz-Asner, Founder of TEAFC, www.TEAFC.org

"The autism community has a thoughtful and dynamic new resource. This book incorporates effective teaching principles for neurodiverse children. Simple language, colorful graphics, and hands-on activities support positive teaching to facilitate successful learning and recall.

Ultimately, this comprehensive approach creates a highly motivating and effective curriculum to promote regulation, attention, body awareness and relaxation through engaging movement and art exercises. A practice CD and bright beautiful illustrations make this a valuable teaching tool that can easily be implemented in home and classroom settings. Yael Calhoun has used her unique insight, experience, and talents to develop a creative and delightful resource that will greatly benefit young children with special needs in wonderful new ways."

~ Lori Krasny, M.S., CCC-SLP

"Yael Calhoun has devoted her life to understanding, helping, and researching children and families with ASD and neurodevelopmental conditions—including appreciating and comprehending foundations for body internalizing, felt sense, developmental movement, neuroception, self-regulation, awareness, and creativity."

~ Louis Allen, MD, FAAP, MPH, Founder of www.ABLE-Differently.org

"*Children's Art and Yoga for Autism and Diverse Abilities* concentrates on what a child can do. It limits excessive vocabulary, is visually-orientated, and is acute to all sensory issues. A true success ... it encompasses all that is positive. This book provides both the classroom teacher and parent tools on how yoga can benefit children not only for the moment but in their daily lives. It provides an alternative way to incorporate yoga and art for children to reach their full potential. Yael Calhoun has a thoughtful and comprehensive approach that really works!!! A wonderful addition to any classroom."

~ Shelley Schwartz, M.A.

"This book is a state-of-the-art resource for anyone who works with children who have autism, special needs, and/or other challenges. The content systematically addresses key skills that we know are essential to strengthen self-regulation, enhance social skills, and build a resilient nervous system. Yael Calhoun's vast experience as an educator and yoga teacher is reflected in how she integrates brain-body strategies with expressive art. The curriculum combines movement, breathing exercises, and art to stimulate brain development and strengthen skills that every child needs to succeed.

In addition, we know that many children with autism and diverse abilities have experienced some type of trauma. A growing body of evidence indicates that working through the body and bottom-up with the brain is essential to trauma recovery. This book, which includes many practical resources, has broad applications in many settings for service providers and families. I will be using it in my work and recommending it to other colleagues."

~ Linda Chamberlain, PhD MPH, Founding Director,
Alaska Family Violence Prevention Project

CHILDREN'S ART and **YOGA** for **AUTISM** and **DIVERSE ABILITIES**

Improve Body Awareness, Sensory Integration, and Emotional Regulation

YAEL CALHOUN

Illustrated by Svea Lunøe

Jessica Kingsley Publishers
London and Philadelphia

The GreenTREE Yoga® Approach:

Building Safety, Supporting Empowerment, and Maintaining Simplicity

*To Sam, Ben, and Alex, who taught me that
neurodiversity is to be celebrated.*

*And to all the children who brought this program
to life with their energy and laughter.*

First published in Great Britain in 2025 by Jessica Kingsley Publishers
An imprint of John Murray Press

1

Copyright © Yael Calhoun 2025
Illustrations © Svea Lunøe 2025
Science figures © Sam Tresco. Many thanks to Sam Tresco, White
Gorge Designs. www.whitegorgedesigns.com

The information contained in this book is not intended to replace the services of trained medical
professionals or to be a substitute for medical advice. The complementary therapy described
in this book may not be suitable for everyone to follow. You are advised to consult a doctor
before embarking on any complementary therapy program and on any matters relating to your
health, and in particular on any matters that may require diagnosis or medical attention.

A CIP catalogue record for this title is available from the British Library and the Library of Congress

ISBN 978 1 83997 830 2
eISBN 978 1 83997 831 9

Printed and bound in the United States by Integrated Books International

Jessica Kingsley Publishers' policy is to use papers that are natural, renewable, and recyclable
products and made from wood grown in sustainable forests. The logging and manufacturing
processes are expected to conform to the environmental regulations of the country of origin.

Jessica Kingsley Publishers
Carmelite House
50 Victoria Embankment
London EC4Y 0DZ

www.jkp.com

John Murray Press
Part of Hodder & Stoughton Ltd
An Hachette Company

The authorised representative in the EEA is Hachette Ireland,
8 Castlecourt Centre, Castleknock Road, Castleknock, Dublin 15, D15 YF6A, Ireland

Contents

Part II: Getting Started

Part III: Building Safety, Supporting Empowerment, and Maintaining Simplicity

Part IV: Set *Yourself* Up for Success

Part V: Teaching the Art and Yoga Curriculum

Part VI: Appendices

Part VII: Supplemental Resources

Acknowledgements

Without the inspiration and contributions of the following people, this project would still be nothing more than notes on my computer, hastily written after summer camps and classroom programs. So it is with much gratitude that I offer each person a special note of thanks for taking the time to identify ways both to inspire and to improve this project. I also want to give you, the parent, teacher, or care provider, a sense of the expertise that these people have offered to guide this program at all stages. It developed over 3 years of pilot projects, reviews, and more programs. This project had a definite beginning, middle, and end, with key people at each point. So, in order of involvement, thank you to ...

GreenTREE Yoga® Board: This group of wonderful people has provided years of strong support to all the GreenTREE projects. Without a committed board, these programs could not have grown and reached so many. A huge and well-deserved thank you for your years of support, each of you lending your expertise and great energy.

Current board: Charlotte Bell, E-RYT; Loren Lambert, Esq.; Hobson Calhoun, MA, MS (our three founding members); Supreet Gill, RYT; and Shelley Schwartz, MA.

Lori Krasny, MS, CCC-SLP: Director of Autism Services (former) at The Children's Center in Salt Lake City: Lori had the vision of bringing children's yoga to her program. We did a pilot, and from there the project gradually became more formalized. Lori's enthusiasm, knowledge, and patience were both inspiring and key to this project. Without Lori's support and encouragement, this program would not have fledged.

Shelley Schwartz, MA, a teacher who devoted her 30-year career to working with autistic children in New York, helped review the CD and the written materials. Guided by her sustained sharing of expertise, I was able to create a CD/DVD and fine-tune the project.

Dawn Young, E-RYT, AYT, worked with me in several of the summer programs, sharing her passion for yoga and her years of experience of working with children of differing abilities, especially children with autism. Dawn also sat on my deck for hours, discussing the program and cutting out triangles and rocket materials for our first camp. Dawn is delightful to watch teach, as she keeps the sense of *lila* (play) alive. She showed me the possibilities.

Carla Anderson, E-RYT, lent her skills in both teaching and editing, making this program much richer. Carla has an uncommon knack for being able to take a big-picture look at a project and yet finely focus on the details. Carla brought a special interest in children with autism to GreenTREE Yoga®, for which I am thankful. Carla read and reread the initial handbook manuscript, each time providing valuable insights and asking strong questions.

Rebecca Carroll, RYT, shared her yoga, teaching, and editing talents as she reviewed this book. Her boundless (and endless) support and clear approach made the program more accessible. A very warm and special thanks to the cheerleader of the group, whose encouragement and keen editing eye are so appreciated.

Scott Anderson, PhD, E-RYT: Scott Anderson developed a wonderful yoga program for children on the spectrum, YogAutism™ (www.yogautism.org). Scott took the time to review the original project on which this book is based and to share his ideas and support. Thank you, Scott, for supporting our original vision with such enthusiasm.

Linda Chamberlain, PhD, MPH, shared her expertise in the field as she reviewed the program and offered insights. In addition, Linda continues to provide ideas about how to bring this resource to more people, demonstrating her continued commitment to sharing the benefits of yoga with diverse and underserved populations. Linda's extensive background in serving underserved populations, creating many books and support materials, and presenting internationally on the issues, provided strong expertise in the review process.

Louis Allen, MD, FAAP: Without Louis' continual, gentle guidance, this program would not have been completed in any sort of timely manner. His nonprofit, ABLE-differently (www.able-differently.org), awarded scholarships for children to attend the summer programs, which allowed us to continue iterating the program. He shared invaluable expertise, vision, and dedication to helping children of differing needs find joy in life. I cannot thank Louis enough for seeing the potential of the project and not letting it go. It greatly helped that I saw him every week at a yoga class—I was greatly inspired to have something new to report to him on the progress! And he was able to ask his gentle questions, "I wonder what it would be like if we ..."

Mona Bingham, PhD, RN, and Margaret Clayton, PhD, APRN, FAAN, reviewed the science chapters. I am continually grateful for their generous sharing of time and expertise to support GreenTREE Yoga® projects. Looking forward to our next project.

Svea Lunøe, RYT: Many special thanks to our illustrator extraordinaire, whose precious and captivating Shanti the Monkey continues to draw children to the magic (well, benefits) of yoga. Thank you for your willingness to draw all that was needed for this project! You continue to bring joy into the lives of people of all ages.

Sam Tresco (www.whitegorgedesigns.com): Many thanks for sharing your artistic talents (science figures) and special energy. And thank you for co-teaching all those kids' yoga classes with me so many years ago when you were a kid.

Many Thanks: I am grateful to the yoga teachers who have used the program and shared their observations with me. Natalie Evershed, RYT, and Erica Nicole, RYT, did some great field testing. Many thanks also to the principals, teachers, parents, and students who allowed me to visit their classrooms and summer camps to share yoga. Without their willingness to try new things, we would be unable to confidently repeat this teacher comment: "This program works well—kids love it!"

Of course, the children who brought this art and yoga program to life deserve special thanks.

And so, to everyone who contributed time and energy and expertise, I hope you are as pleased as I am with how our shared efforts came together.

A celebration of synergy!

Namaste,

Yael Calhoun

Introduction

Children's Art and Yoga for Autism and Diverse Abilities is a trauma-informed resource for anyone developing a program to teach children with physical, emotional, behavioral, or mental challenges. Quite simply, this book's intention aligns to support, as Barry Prizant, PhD, writes in *Uniquely Human*, "creating a life of positive memories. We can do that when we offer choices instead of exerting control, whenever we foster the child's interests and honor the child's strengths ... whenever we make learning, work, and life fun and joyful."[1] *Art and Yoga* is an inclusive program with sensitivity to the many processing issues these children may experience. Rather than write specifically about each condition with the evolving terms and definitions, this book provides general guidance on how to set up and to adapt programs to meet the changing needs of your group. In addition, conditions can also co-occur. This book does provide background information on autism and sensory processing considerations. It is a book I wish I had as a resource when Lori Krasny, MS, CCC-SLP, who ran an autism program for 60 children, came to my workshop on self-care. She said, "You have to come and do this yoga with our children." I told her I knew nothing about autism. She said that she would teach me. And she did.

While conditions or diagnoses are varied and can change, what remains a constant is the need for vigilance in how you teach, in how you set up the room, and in how you demonstrate continued sensitivity to differing abilities and learning styles. The good news is you do not need a specialized degree to share this program. You do need a willingness to collaborate with parents or professionals who understand the ability levels of their child or group. You may be working with an individual, a class of mixed abilities, or a class of more able children. Therefore, the suggestion is to use an appropriate collaborative process that can include teachers, clinicians, and parents/caregivers.

This art and yoga program is based on the trauma-informed GreenTREE Yoga® Approach of building safety, supporting empowerment, and maintaining simplicity. Stephen Porges, PhD, has written on the importance of building safety in his many foundational books on polyvagal theory. His ideas serve as a clear guide to this program. Safety is a key to working with anyone in need of learning self-regulation skills. Therefore, a recurring theme in this book is that to learn, someone needs to feel safe. It's body physiology. The yoga practices in this book can also be used as a stand-alone program for these groups. There may be times when sharing the yoga program without the art component is a better fit.

> **Trauma-informed** does not mean that you are informed about someone's personal trauma. Trauma-informed does mean that an organization, program, or person is informed about the effects of trauma. What does that mean? Trauma can change the way the brain functions at the cellular level. These changes can affect someone's ability to process language and the way someone responds to various stimuli. All GreenTREE Yoga® programs are trauma-informed and are designed using science-based protocols. Why? As this book will show, there is much benefit to teaching children with diverse learning styles in a trauma-informed way.

The book chapters are designed to support your efforts to build a flexible program, the benefits of which can extend well beyond the class time. The art and yoga program can lay the groundwork for short yoga breaks both children and parents can practice at home or at school. To support your teaching efforts, this book introduces some simple science to both inform and inspire your program development. The scripts, charts, art projects, and many supplemental resources (SR) provide easy-to-follow and easy-to-adapt ideas and suggestions.

Let's consider all this book provides.

Part I: Simple Science

Presents the science that guides this art and yoga program.

Chapter 1 begins with brain basics, starting with nerve cells and building to the triune model of the brain. From that simple science can come an appreciation of what may be happening in the brains of those with differing learning styles.

Chapter 2 offers a brief introduction to what stress does to both the body and brain. It then introduces Stephen Porges' polyvagal theory and provides more reasons to take care in planning and teaching your classes. It may also inspire you to read Part IV on self-care (taking care of you).

Chapter 3 discusses what it means to have differing abilities and learning styles. Sections on autism spectrum disorder (ASD) and sensory processing disorders (SPDs) complete the chapter.

Chapter 4 discusses the science of yoga as a healing tool. It includes the simple science of safety, of breathing, and of movement. What may be unexpected is a discussion on the science of fun and play. Children's yoga needs to be fun, and there is science to explain its importance. The chapter ends with a section on learning: not because it is least important, but because it is most important. Children need to learn a wide variety of things: from facts to social skills, to physical movements, to self-regulation skills and appropriate behaviors. A program that can adapt to different learning styles while building a sense of safety is a strong part of empowering a child to learn. Again, it is body physiology.

Part II: Getting Started

Chapter 5 discusses how to promote your program, how to organize the yoga, and as importantly, how to organize the art project. Organization makes your program easier to teach. It also keeps your program predictable and consistent, which eases the stress of transitions for children.

Part III: Building Safety, Supporting Empowerment, and Maintaining Simplicity

Each chapter focuses on one part of the GreenTREE Yoga® Approach.

Chapter 6 discusses how you can build a sense of safety, which is the primary consideration. Clear categories to consider are: 1) the room; 2) sensory stimuli; 3) your teaching intentions around building safety; and 4) the value of interactive teaching. This last section discusses the social engagement system, adapting to the needs of your group, and the value of fun and play. Again, fun and play are not last because they are least important. Rather, fun and play make up the final note to stress their importance in any children's yoga program. Quite simply, your program needs to be fun. And it can be fun without sensory overload.

Chapter 7 discusses many simple ways you can support empowering a child. These approaches include: 1) the power of choice; 2) the power of positive phrasing and pauses; 3) the power of building physical strength; and 4) the power of normalization.

Chapter 8 provides many ideas on how you can maintain simplicity in your program. With differing abilities and learning styles, simplicity is of critical importance. If children are confused by your language, poses, and instructions, they may *feel* anxious, frustrated, or disengaged. At that point, you are not building a sense of safety or supporting empowerment. This section gives many ideas on how you can maintain simplicity using three strategies: 1) simple language; 2) simple yoga and simple breathwork; and 3) simple verbal instructions paired with simple visual cues. If you set a child up for success, you set them up for being more able to learn. This learning includes adaptive strategies for managing stress and frustration.

Part IV: Set *Yourself* Up for Success

Provides an often-overlooked component to setting children up for success: taking care of yourself. Quite simply, self-care means you can bring your best self to the program.

Chapter 9 offers ideas on how to take care of you, including short yoga and breathwork breaks for you to do at home or at work. Free downloads of audio, video, and handouts of these breaks to help you manage your stress levels are included. The suggestion is to give yourself some time to consider the ideas in this chapter.

Chapter 10 outlines simple ways to build your confidence in teaching this program. After reading about the importance of the social engagement system in helping children learn to self-regulate, you can appreciate the many opportunities to use how you sound and even your facial expressions as teaching tools. Practicing the four simple steps outlined in the chapter, complete with practice scripts, can set you up for a more confident and enjoyable teaching experience.

Part V: Teaching the Art and Yoga Curriculum

Chapter 11 considers two key questions: 1) Why would you want to teach this program? 2) What are the benefits?

Chapter 12 provides a key step in developing your program. The chapter is framed around teaching intentions consistent with the GreenTREE Yoga® Approach. It provides easy-to-use tables of suggested phrases used in the teaching scripts.

Chapter 13 describes the five-part class format: 1) the Hello Song; 2) yoga; 3) art project; 4) more yoga, including the pose of the day; and 5) the Goodbye Song.

Chapter 14 provides background information on the teaching scripts, followed by the text for the 1-hour practice scripts. The yoga component can be taught as a stand-alone program, with the option of adding art projects later.

Chapter 15 outlines the six art projects, listing materials and instructions.

Part VI: Appendices

These resources, as outlined in the table of contents, can support your program development and teaching.

Part VII: Supplemental Resources (SR)

This section directs you to free materials that you can download and share.

Please consult your health care professional if you have any questions about your child's or your group's ability to practice simple stretching or breathing exercises. This book only provides suggestions for your consideration and is **not** offering medical advice.

PART I

SIMPLE SCIENCE

CHAPTER 1

Brain Basics

It makes sense to begin a discussion of how you can make a positive difference for children with autism and other physical, emotional, and mental challenges by talking about the brain. This art and yoga program is designed to create connections. Connecting movement, the breath, and the mind supports children in developing more adaptive strategies. What strategies would be helpful for these groups? Strategies for handling stress, building physical strength, strengthening social skills, and having fun. Meeting these intentions comes back to what is happening (or not happening) in a child's brain. These ideas may be new to you or may serve as a quick review.

Neurons

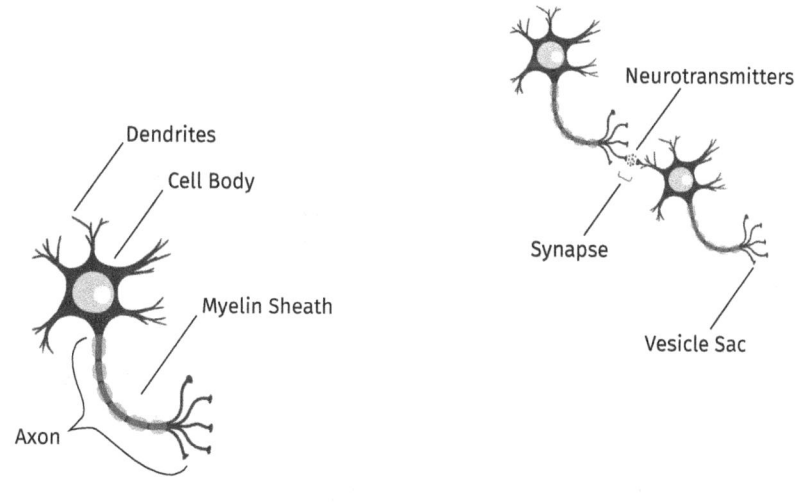

FIGURE 1.1: A NEURON

You may have noticed the terms *neuro*typical and *neuro*divergent begin with *neuro*, from the Latin word *neuro* meaning nerves or nervous system. We will circle back to the importance of these words, but let's start with what a typical, healthy neuron is and how it works.

A neuron is a nerve cell. These nerve cells send and receive signals throughout the body and brain (Figure 1.1). A neuron has several parts, including the cell body, the dendrites, and the axons. Chemical and electrical signals are sent via the axons and are received by other neurons through the dendrites. Axons are covered with myelin sheaths, fatty coverings that act like insulation and can affect how quickly signals are sent. Neurons have vesicle sacs at the end of the axons. These sacs secrete neurotransmitters (chemical messengers). Neurotransmitters carry the messages across the gaps between the neurons (synapses). Some commonly known neurotransmitters are dopamine, serotonin, and acetylcholine.

Types of Neurons

There are two types of neurons: sensory and motor neurons. As you can tell from the name, sensory neurons send messages to the different parts of the brain about what we sense. These senses include what we taste, touch, hear, smell, and see. Motor neurons then send signals from the brain (upper motor neurons) or spinal cord (lower motor neurons) to muscles. Motor neurons control both voluntary and involuntary movements. But we process even more signals from what are sometimes called the hidden senses: the vestibular system and the proprioceptive system. These senses give us perceptions of speed, movement, pressure on joints and muscles, and where our body is in space.[1] The vestibular system is in the inner ear and senses movement and changes in the position of the head. It has been shown to contribute to multisensory integration.[2] [3] Quite simply, it helps to organize incoming sensory information so we can respond appropriately. The proprioceptive system provides feedback to the brain about where our body is in relation to itself and the outside world. We also use this sense to gauge how tightly to hold something or how much to tighten our muscles to move.[4] Research as to how these different systems work together is ongoing.

Waiting for the Doorbell: Let's consider a simple example. Imagine that you are sitting at home waiting for someone. The doorbell rings. You answer the door. Let's run that through the sensory travel log. First, perhaps a sight or sound alerted you to the door. Your vestibular system aided in the balance and coordination of moving from a seated to standing position. Your proprioception system helped organize your movements: one foot forward, other foot forward, your arm out to open the door, and your hand pressing down on the handle hard enough to open. Many senses provided input that was sorted and organized in different parts of the brain. Then the responses (your thoughts and movements) were coordinated as motor neurons sent signals back from the brain to muscles. One more example to try if you like, as it's an important point to understand in working with children with differing needs. As you read this sentence: 1) pick up a pencil; 2) raise that arm out to the side; 3) look at your hand; and 4) shake that hand without dropping the pencil. Can you track your sensory travel log? As you are reading these words and looking at your hand, how many of your senses are sending signals? These signals all provide information to your brain. Return signals to your muscles coordinate a physical response: first to raise your arm to the side and then to hold the pencil firmly enough so you don't drop it while shaking your hand.

Living Cells: While that process may seem straightforward, these signals are being sent by living cells. And neurons can undergo changes before birth and all through the life span. Genetic and environmental factors can affect how neurons live, function, change, and die. Neurons can also become damaged and undergo repair. If it sounds complicated, it's because it is. As neurons send and receive chemical and electrical signals, there are many places for disruptions and changes in signaling to occur. But before we discuss disruptions, let's look at how these neurons function in a typical, healthy brain.

The Triune Brain

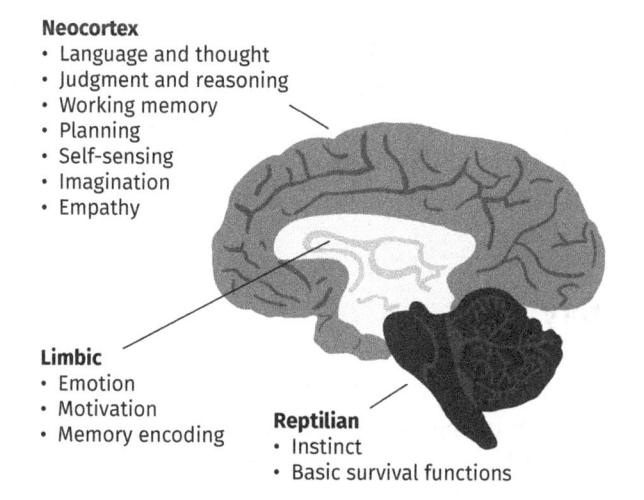

FIGURE I.2: THE TRIUNE BRAIN

A useful model is the triune brain proposed in the 1960s by Paul MacLean, MD.[5] It's a simple model that gives a general idea of what is going on in a typical brain. The triune brain has three parts: 1) the reptilian (or lizard brain); 2) the limbic; and 3) the neocortex. Figure 1.2 provides a quick outline of the functions. The reptilian brain regulates vital survival body functions we do not need to think about, including breathing, heartbeat, and body temperature. Imagine if to stay alive, we had to think about taking about every breath. We take over 20,000 breaths in a day. The limbic system, often called the emotional part of the brain, includes the parts where we assess and respond to threats and where memories are first encoded. The third part of the triune brain is the neocortex, the thinking or rational portion of the brain. Neurons continually carry signals to and from the body and brain. Signals also travel among the different parts of the brain for processing and responses. It's important to know that brain research and discovery are ongoing. That idea is worth repeating. The way a typical brain works and all its connections are still being studied. What does all this science mean for art and yoga?

Are We Stuck?

Here is the piece of this discussion that highlights the many possibilities for healing and improving physical, emotional, and mental functions. These living cells (neurons) can change in ways that can help children with differing needs. And these changes in the brain can happen based on what a child thinks, what a child does, or both. Let's spend a few minutes on the idea of *neuro*plasticity. There is that word again: *neuro* (neuron). To be plastic means being capable of change. It is interesting to note that estimates from the 2023 Brain Atlas (21 papers published in the journal *Science*) hold that the human brain has an estimated 3,300 different types of brain cells, for a total of 170 billion. About half of these are neurons.[6] That is many opportunities for change. There is a fascinating history in the study of how our brains can change.

A Bit of History

Current neuroscience researchers can use brain images to see: 1) how different signals are fired; 2) which parts of the brain are active during a thought or an action; and 3) how brain signaling and the brain itself can change. Sigmund Freud, MD, Moshé Feldenkrais, PhD, William James, PhD, Ramón y Cajal, PhD, and other foundational thinkers and researchers had discussed these ideas for many years before neuroimaging technology existed. In the late 1800s, William James, often called the father of American psychology, coined the term *plasticity*, which later led to the term *neuroplasticity*, meaning the brain's ability to change.[7] In 1906, one of the first Nobel Prizes was won by Ramón y Cajal, who studied the structure of the nervous system. Later, Eric Kandel, MD, showed that two things create conditions for neuroplastic changes: how we think about something and what we physically do (mental and physical actions).[8] He was awarded the 1990 Nobel Prize for these ideas. *The Brain That Changes Itself: Stories of Personal Triumph from the Frontiers of Brain Science* by Norman Doidge, MD, provides discussions on how these changes can happen and provides heartening real-life examples.[9]

A Note: We know that the young brain is the most capable of neuroplastic change. Jeffrey S. Anderson, MD, PhD, is a neuroscientist who studies brain connectivity issues. Quite simply, he studies the way the parts of the brain connect to each other and to other parts of the body. Of relevance to our discussion is his belief that the earlier the intervention, the greater the potential for affecting an autistic person's life.[10]

CHAPTER 2

Stress, Polyvagal Theory, and Self-Regulation

When you get upset or gear up for a big task and then later find calm, you are experiencing your stress cycle. The stress cycle is a physiological feedback loop enabling us to get ready for action when we need to and then to rest. This ability to get excited or to calm down is the ability to self-regulate. Before we circle back to this key idea, we need a bit more stress science to understand what we are regulating.

The Stress Cycle

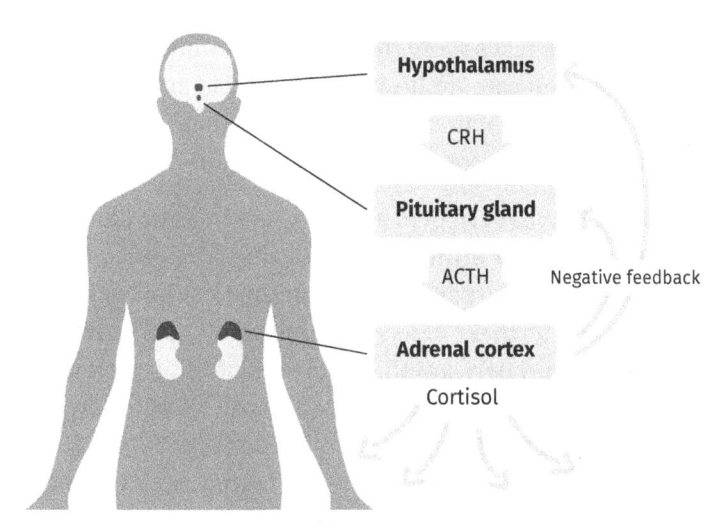

FIGURE 2.1: THE HPA AXIS

Stress Loops: The stress feedback loop is called the hypothalamic-pituitary-adrenal (HPA) axis (Figure 2.1). We get stressed. Our body secretes stress hormones (epinephrine or adrenaline, cortisol, and norepinephrine) so we can respond to the stress or perceived danger. In the short term, this response is a good thing. It improves our immune function, improves our ability to focus, and gives us more energy. Then, in a healthy system, the stress loop resets itself when the danger has passed.

Stuck in a Loop: But what if we don't feel the danger has passed? Then that *feeling* of danger or anxiety has become chronic stress. Chronic stress, or the body being flooded with stress hormones, has a robust list of negative physical and emotional effects. Such long-term basic needs as digestion, reproduction, sleeping, immune function, learning, and healing are compromised. Did you notice that learning is on that list? Another effect is that the thinking part of the brain can be impaired. Or, quite simply, we don't think well or make rational decisions. We are in survival mode, which is the nonverbal, non-thinking part of the brain. This expression is body physiology: "I am so upset I can't think straight."

High Road or Low Road? A relevant point for anyone struggling with emotional control or behavioral issues is that it's about timing. Joseph Ledoux, PhD, a neuroscientist, uses the expressions high road and low road to describe different response times.[1] What does that mean? It means that it takes more time for a signal to travel to the thinking part of the brain for a thoughtful response than it takes for an emotional response. Emotional response happens quickly, no thought involved. So, thinking about the consequences of having a fit or hitting someone takes more time than the simple no-thought reaction of hitting someone. You can see how first *practicing* and then *learning* some self-regulation techniques can support creating that extra time needed for someone to manage their responses.

Stress Signals: Well, what triggers a feeling of stress or danger in the first place? Again, taking a few minutes to read this section could inform and inspire how you teach this art and yoga program. Let's go back to the sensory neurons that help us to make sense of things. How does that work? Well, that's the key question. There are three sources of information that sensory neurons first detect and then send as signals to the brain for processing. One source is what is happening outside of us (exteroception). Is the room hot, noisy, crowded, too bright, smelly, or messy? Is that person too close to me? A second source of information comes from inside of us (interoception): Are my hands cold, am I hungry, does my stomach hurt, or is my heart pounding? Difficulties with sensory signals can lead to difficulties in self-regulation.

Neuroception: Stephen Porges, PhD, describes a third source of information, which he terms *neuro*ception.[2] There is the word *neuro* again. Some people call this intuition or a gut feeling. An interesting side note is that 80 percent of neurons outside of the brain are in the gut. Neuroception is information that is perceived or sensed without words in the nonverbal (subcortical) part of the brain. These cues may come from within the body or from something outside of the body. Some expressions reflect this idea: feeling gut-punched or having a sick feeling in the pit of your stomach. That *feeling* may be one you can't explain in words because the signals are processed in the nonverbal parts of the brain. We will circle back to this idea as the basis of this important guide to teaching: Show, Don't Tell. Quite simply, it means teaching in a way that allows someone to experience *feeling* safe. Telling someone who isn't fully using the verbal parts of their brain, "You are safe here," or "You will feel better," isn't setting them up for success. If safety is the issue, which it is, your challenge is to help someone to *feel* safe.

Adults collect sensory data in these three ways. Children can also collect sensory data in these same three ways. Keep this front and center in the thinking and planning part of your brain (the neocortex) when we discuss ideas on how to set up your room for art and for yoga.

Polyvagal Theory, Social Engagement, and Self-Regulation

Stephen Porges first published his ideas on polyvagal theory in 1994. His work continues to be widely recognized for the scientific clarity and guidance it brings to healing and teaching protocols.[3] A quick look at this foundational theory could also inspire some of your teaching approaches and your self-care protocols discussed in Part IV. Why? Because we can offer everyone simple tools to manage stress levels. They can first *practice* and then *learn* more adaptive stress management strategies.

Polyvagal Theory: Dr. Porges' polyvagal theory provides a much-needed update to the simple model of our autonomic nervous system as an on/off or hot/cold system. The on-switch is the sympathetic nervous system, known as the fight-or-flight or freeze response. The off-switch is the parasympathetic nervous system, the rest-and-digest feature. Signals sent between the body and the brain and back again travel along the tenth cranial nerve, which Charles Darwin called the pneumogastric nerve. Figure 2.2 shows the many points of connection, which explains why the tenth cranial nerve is called the vagus (Greek for wandering) nerve.

Dr. Porges explains in his many books and papers that this bidirectional nerve, the polyvagal nerve, creates the brain-heart connection.[4] The reason that feelings of stress or fear or anxiety come across in your voice or facial expression is because these pathways connect the vagus nerve to the muscles in the throat (larynx) and face. This science is yet another reason to practice how you sound (Chapter 10). It's an invaluable teaching tool for your program. Speaking of how you sound brings us to another of Dr. Porges' key ideas.

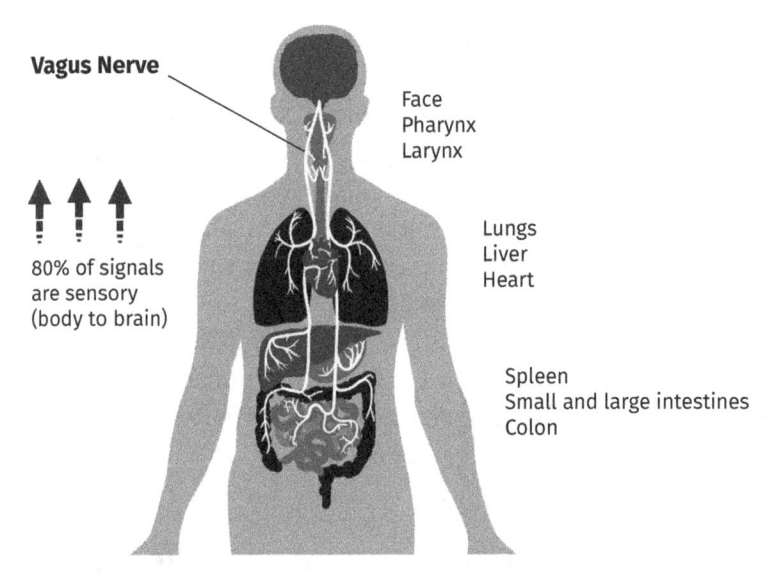

FIGURE 2.2: THE VAGUS NERVE

The Social Engagement System: Dr. Porges presents the idea of a third layer of the nervous system function: the social engagement system.[5] Mammals can override fight-or-flight or freeze responses by reading safety cues from other mammals. Safety cues come from sounds and facial expressions. Think about the effects of a soothing voice/an angry voice; a cheerful face/an upset face; supportive words/judgmental words; or a purr/a growl. Fortunately, you have been fine-tuning your social engagement system for years. You continually adjust your voice, perhaps talking, chanting, or singing. You may use another type of language, perhaps sign or body language. Think about your facial expression when you are trying to offer comfort: That's social engagement. Breathing or moving with someone, perhaps modeling long, slow breaths out that can lower heart rate and lower blood pressure, is social engagement. Common sense and experience tell us that dogs, horses, or cats (whether service animals or family pets) can also help someone to override a stress response.

As someone with a variety of communications skills and facial expressions, you have a lot with which to work. Why does it matter? Because again, and again, how safe someone feels directly affects their ability to learn (rewire their brain) so that interacting with the world is a more positive part of their day.

It matters because social engagement can set someone up first to *practice* and then to *learn* self-regulation skills.

Self-regulation: Self-regulation is a common term. Children with differing abilities and learning styles often have challenges with self-regulation. What does that mean? Self-regulation is the ability to manage such stressful feelings as frustration, anger, or anxiety. Again, it's the ability to bring your nervous system back from fight-or-flight or freeze to a calmer state. Practicing self-regulation is a practice of moving through stressful feelings, but it is also the ability to move out of feeling collapsed or shut down. If someone has poor self-regulation skills, they may immediately become dysregulated (angry, oppositional, avoidant, or shut down) when stressed. And understanding that it's a quick and automatic response provides your starting point.

Your core teaching intention should be building skills to help these children (and their families) stay regulated. As Barry Prizant, PhD, notes in his 2015/2022 book *Uniquely Human*, this difficulty to stay emotionally and physiologically regulated has long been overlooked by professionals who have focused on behaviors instead of underlying causes.[6] That idea is worth rereading. We will discuss the fact that how you set up the room, how you plan the activities, and how you manage the people in that room can affect stress levels. A child's dysregulated response to what they perceive as something out of control or disorganized can cause behavior issues. Your starting point, then, is being aware of some underlying causes of dysregulated responses: making sure the room is not a mess; the activities are not scattered; the sounds in the room are not dissonant or overwhelming; and people are not moving in unpredictable ways. The starting point is being aware of stress triggers so you set children up for success: *practicing* adaptive responses (self-regulation to build a sense of safety) that can then become *learned* (a habit). We will come back to these important ideas throughout this book.

CHAPTER 3

Differing Abilities and Neurodiversity

It makes sense to begin and to end this chapter with the same key idea. That key idea is we do not have to fully understand the brains of children with differing abilities and learning styles to create a program sensitive to their processing and physical considerations. We can look for programs that use what neuroscience, researchers and practitioners in the field, and parents have identified as challenges for these diverse groups. Some behaviors and challenges are common to many of these conditions. Let's take a broad view of differing abilities.

Differing Abilities

There are a wide range of physical, behavioral, emotional, and mental challenges that children can experience. This book's use of the term differing needs or abilities includes, but it is not limited to, autism spectrum disorder (ASD), Down syndrome, visual and auditory impairments, Tourette's, sensory processing disorders (SPD), attention deficit hyperactivity disorder (ADHD), attention deficit disorder (ADD), dyslexia, schizophrenia, bipolar disorder, obsessive compulsive disorder (OCD), and a variety of other physical, behavioral/emotional, and mental challenges.

While it is not within the scope of this book to define each condition, a broad overview can be useful. More information on some of these conditions is available in the 'Resources: Books, Websites, Podcasts' section and in Louise Goldberg's informative book, *Yoga Therapy for Children with Autism and Special Needs* (2013).

Some Working Definitions: The Americans with Disabilities Act was amended in 2008 to define disability as a physical or mental impairment that substantially limits one or more major life activities of such an individual.[1] In Down syndrome (trisomy 21), an extra 21st chromosome is in some or all genes. Typically, a person has 23 pairs of chromosomes. Down's children may have poor muscle tone, delayed mental and social development, and other physical, emotional, and mental challenges. Emotional or behavioral disorders (EBD) can present as children being anxious, disruptive, oppositional, avoidant, or compulsive.[2] Autism spectrum disorder (ASD) has had a long and noteworthy history, discussed in more detail in the next section.

Too Much Information: An occupational therapist and psychologist, A. Jean Ayres, PhD, OTR, identified the impact of sensory processing disorders (SPDs) on the behaviors of children, many with other disorders as well.[3] Children can have sensory integration challenges that can cause some visual and physical disruptions. One example is an inability to relay or process sensory information (something they hear or see) into a controlled behavior or a planned series of movements (responding easily or in an appropriate way).[4] [5] They may also have a hypersensitivity to smell, sounds, or touch.[6] We will circle back to SPD later in this chapter. Considering these conditions and disorders leads us to a discussion of the term neurodiversity.

Neurodiversity

To support those working to improve the lives of these children and their families, let's consider the term neurodiversity. That term offers a less stigmatizing and more inclusive way of looking at differing abilities. Again, *neuro* means nerve. Interestingly, the term neurodiversity was coined by Judy Singer, PhD, at the time an Australian graduate student who brought her lifetime of personal experiences with autism to her academic research.[7] Neurodiversity highlights the diversity of human brain functions. Some brains are typical (*neuro*typical), and some brains are quite different (that is, they diverge) from what is typical. What does that mean? Everyone's brain works in unique ways, shaped by both genetic factors and environmental influences. A useful analogy is to think of the neuronal signals creating wires through which information moves. *Neuro*divergent means that in some ways there are signaling or routing issues. Quite simply, sometimes the signals get crossed or get too strong or don't happen at all. Let's look at two examples of *neuro*divergence that illustrate this point. Then let's look at what neurodivergent thought has given society.

When Sight Becomes a Taste: One fascinating example of how signals can get crossed is a condition called synesthesia (or synaesthesia). It is from the Greek root words *syn*, meaning union, and *aesthesis*, meaning sensation. Individuals may hear music, yet they see shapes. Or they may hear their name and see a color. Other senses can be included in the mix. Someone might see a shape, but they experience a distinct taste instead. In his fascinating 2022 book, *The Man Who Tasted Words*, the neurologist Guy Leschziner, PhD, says what it is clear is that synesthesia fundamentally alters the way people experience the world.[8] And before you dismiss the condition as almost nonexistent, studies suggest that 1 in 20 people may experience some part of the more than 150 different types of synesthesia.[9]

Looking at a Brain as It Works: An example of too many signals getting sent is offered by Temple Grandin, PhD, a professor, researcher, and writer who has contributed foundational work to the study of autism. She has had much neuroimaging done on her autistic brain to further the field of study. It was discovered that her amygdalae (a paired structure) were enlarged.[10] The amygdalae are part of the limbic system, the emotional part of the triune brain. It's primarily involved in processing emotions and memories associated with fear. This information was helpful to her as she tried to understand and manage her overactive fight-or-flight system.

Advances in neuroscience (including such neuroimaging techniques as MRIs and fMRIs) have allowed researchers to identify some neurological patterns in various disorders. Such science has put to rest the ideas that these conditions signal mental deficiencies or mental illness. Let's look at some numbers. Then we can consider the history that led to our current time of greater understanding and profound changes in protocols to support those with differing abilities and learning styles.

Neurodiversity and Gifts to Society: I taught college environmental biology and was an environmental planner, so the term biodiversity came to my mind as a way to grasp the importance of neurodiversity. Quite simply, biodiversity is the variety all living things. We have observed that a system with biodiversity (from genes to species to ecosystems) is a healthier, more resilient biological system. With that in mind, let's consider examples of the gifts that neurodiversity has given to society. As we continue to study both biodiversity and neurodiversity, the wonders are still being explored.

In her 2022 book, *Visual Thinking*, Temple Grandin, PhD, entitles a chapter: Genius and Neurodiversity. It is an intriguing discussion of some science and history of those who have contributed greatness in their fields. While some have been formally diagnosed as being neurodivergent, historical figures can only be called neurodivergent thinkers based on anecdotes or biographies. Dr. Grandin includes relevant discussions about the lives of Michelangelo, Thomas Edison, Alan Turing, Pablo Picasso, Bill Gates, Steve Jobs, Mark

Zuckerberg, Steven Spielberg, Albert Einstein, Gustave Flaubert, and William Butler Yeats. It's a fascinating chapter that I encourage you to explore. For example, Einstein's teacher told his mother the boy was addled. Dr. Grandin observes that what seems to be a common theme is these people had the ability to explore, combined with a certain perseverance and single-mindedness. She concludes that these traits, combined with divergent thinking that is visual, are "the hallmarks of brilliant innovators."[11]

Obviously, not every neurodivergent thinker is a genius. But hopefully the gift of thinking differently is becoming more appreciated. Steve Silberman noted a call he received from a supervisor at Microsoft, who told him that most of his top programmers (debuggers) are autistic. They can hold hundreds of lines of code as a visual image in the mind and look for mistakes.[12] Perhaps the message from these thoughts is that taking the time to learn how you can support neurodivergent children and their families is time well spent. Supporting neurodiversity supports a healthier society.

Autism

The Numbers: Although there are wide ranges of expressions of neurodiversity, we're going to focus on autism as a condition because many of us are likely to encounter someone with autism. In the United States, a 2023 government report stated that 1 in 36 aged 8-year-old children (approximately 4% of boys and 1% of girls) was estimated to be on the autism spectrum in 2020.[13] This number is a big change from the 1 in 88 children reported by the Centers for Disease Control (CDC) in 2012.[14] It's a remarkable change from the 1 in 1,000 children reported in the 1980s.[15] A new study suggests that the total autistic population could be over 1.2 million in England alone, nearly twice the previously cited figure for the entire UK.[16] What's happening? It's not an outbreak of autism but more likely reflects changes in how autism is screened for and diagnosed.

The Definition: Autism spectrum disorder (ASD) is now defined in the fifth edition of the Diagnostic and Statistical Manual of Mental Disorders (DSM-5) as a neurodevelopmental disorder characterized by deficits in social communication and by restricted interests and repetitive behaviors.[17] The definition was amended in 2020 with no significant changes.[18] The DSM-5 groups all the subcategories of autism under one umbrella term, autism spectrum disorder. But arriving at this definition was a long road with many unfortunate and harmful stops.

The Long Road to the Autism Spectrum: Autism has been studied and written about for over a hundred years. The idea of calling autism a disorder was put forth by a German psychiatrist, Eugen Bleuler, in 1911.[19] He applied the term to the most severe cases of schizophrenia, another one of his diagnostic ideas. The term autism is from the Greek word *autos*, meaning self. In 1943, Leo Kanner, MD, a child psychiatrist, deemed autism a psychiatric condition, calling the pattern of behaviors early infantile autism.[20] This idea continued through the 1950s and 1960s, with Bruno Bettelheim, MD, adding to the misinformation by blaming autistic children on their refrigerator mothers.[21]

Asperger's and Beyond: In a lecture on autism in 1938, the Austrian physician, Hans Asperger, MD, identified a group of highly intelligent children who showed autistic characteristics. He called them little professors.[22] His findings remained untranslated until the work of Lorna Wing, PhD, a researcher at the Medical Research Council in Camberwell, London. Dr. Wing translated and used Dr. Asperger's research to craft her broader argument that autism should be understood as a spectrum of disorders, some very different from each other but sharing genetic similarities or roots. Dr. Wing said in an interview with *The Guardian*: "One of my favorite sayings is that nature never draws a line without smudging it. You cannot separate into those with and without traits. They are so scattered."[23] She took a large step forward in efforts to support families and professionals by coining the term autism spectrum. The term brought a more positive connotation to the term autism, one that brought with it images of rainbows and creativity in nature.[24]

The Autism Square: Dr. Wing and her colleague Judith Gould, PhD, identified a triad of impairments, now expanded to a square with the addition of fourth factor: 1) disturbed mutual contact; 2) disturbed mutual communication; 3) limited imagination; and 4) limited planning ability. As Judy Singer notes, the use of this term rescues people from being seen as having poor characters, bad personalities, and even more defects by showing that their behaviors are based in neurological differences.[25]

If You've Met One Person with Autism … Stephen Shore, PhD, is credited with saying that if you've met one person with autism, you've met one person with autism. Researchers now consider autism to be a cluster of underlying conditions, not one thing. These conditions can present as a constellation of behaviors that may show in different ways at different stages of development.[26] If that sounds complicated, it is because it is complicated. Oliver Sacks, MD, a brilliant physician, neurologist, and author, wrote in *An Anthropologist on Mars*: "No two people with autism are ever the same: Its precise form or expression is different in every case."[27] Unlike Down syndrome, which is an aberration on one gene, autism has been shown to have a strong and varied genetic component. One researcher, Craig Newschaffer, PhD, at Johns Hopkins School of Medicine, estimates that 60–90 percent of autism in twins can be explained by genetics.[28] A 2020 report in *Journal of the American Medicine Association (JAMA) Psychiatry* found that genetic factors consistently played a larger role than environmental factors in autism.[29] A 2020 study published in *Cell* identified 102 risk genes for autism.[30] Others have concluded that this variety of genetic expressions can explain the vast differences in autism.[31] Research tells us that autism is not a result of things society has done, but rather it has genetic markers from deep in our past.[32]

The Social Engagement System Revisited: Stephen Porges notes the cluster of autism traits can include poor eye gaze (gaze aversion); difficulty extracting human voice from background noises (noise/auditory hypersensitivity); speech delays; blunted facial expressions (poor social skills); minimal head gestures; and limited vocal prosody (vocal tones and intonations).[33] [34] He also includes poor emotional state regulation as another trait common in autism. Again, and again, successful programming comes back to building a sense of safety so someone can learn to self-regulate. Successful programming comes back to body physiology and understanding underlying causes.

Be Part of the Solution: Dr. Grandin has observed three basic categories in these specialized brains. There are visual thinkers, as she is. There are music and math thinkers who think in patterns. And there are verbal logic thinkers who think in word details. Visual and verbal thinking exist along a continuum of spatial visualizers and object visualizers.[35] [36] Again, autism is not one thing and there is not one learning style. As science has shown, genetics may be the starting point, but there are changes in someone's environment that can support their efforts to create better lives.[37] You can be part of that support by better understanding that the children in your room arrive with a host of diverse learning styles and processing considerations. What does that mean? It means one last stop before we look at how you can provide some support with this art and yoga program.

Sensory Processing Disorders

We come back to sensory processing disorder (SPD). While SPD is not diagnosed as a separate condition, sensory concerns are widely understood to be an underpinning to neurodivergent experiences. Therefore, a basic understanding of various sensory differences can make any program stronger. Current numbers are from 5 to 17 percent of the general population have SPD symptoms.[38] [39] One study in the *American Journal of Occupational Therapy* showed that 95 percent of children with autism demonstrated some degree of sensory processing dysfunction.[40] For some biological reason, the way sensory information is sent or processed in the brain is too much, resulting in hypersensitivity. Let's look at the senses and what these and other processing issues can look (or *feel*) like. Quite simply, what is someone's day like for them? And how can you improve their experiences for that day?

Sound: I was doing a family yoga program at a public library. We had always had great fun when I suggested we all roar like a mama lion trying to call her cub, which can be heard up to 5 miles away. But that day, a little boy clapped his hands over his ears and got very upset. It was before my art and yoga program, and I had no idea about auditory concerns in neurodivergent brains. Misophonia is a condition in which someone is highly sensitive to or triggered by such sounds as chewing, tapping, or even breathing. These hypersensitivities to sounds, voices, and background noises can be the result of damage to the middle ear muscles, damage to neural pathways in the auditory nerve, or damage to some central brain structures. This damage can also be found in those who have experienced trauma.[41] Again, it's complicated. But I hadn't needed to know the science. All I had needed to know was that differences in how sound is processed can cause great distress if loud or sudden noises occur. All I had needed to know was that teaching *soft* lion roars (or yawns) was the way to teach lion pose. For those interested in learning more about decreasing hypersensitivity (that is, rewiring the brain in a more adaptive way), Stephen Porges' Safe and Sound Listening Protocol might be of interest.[42] It is research-based and designed to build a sense of safety and social engagement through sounds.

Smell: Smell is another sense to which someone can hypersensitive. Sometimes smell detection gives too much sensory information. Then consider that these smell signals go to the thalamus (limbic system), where the signals immediately get sent to the amygdalae (limbic system) for responses. A fun fact: Smell is the only sense that does not first get routed to the neocortex, the thinking part of the brain, for processing. So, we smell something. The amygdalae mount the response. This short sensory pathway (again, not getting routed to the rational part of the brain first) makes smells a potent trigger. Interestingly, for those who have experienced trauma, smell can also be a strong trigger. Again, you don't have to understand the brain science of why someone is hypersensitive to smells. You should, however, be informed that smells (including food, flowers, mats, and essential oils) in the room are an important consideration and set up your room accordingly.

Sight: In sighted individuals, what we see sets up another set of sensory signals along pathways from the optic nerve to the visual cortex, where processing and responses then occur. Again, all of this happens as neurons send and receive signals. Let's consider some examples. Seeing a messy room, someone with a *neuro*typical brain might think, "This room is a mess." That's it, and they go on with the day. They may not even notice the flickering overhead fluorescent lights. They can easily read the writing on a screen across the room. But in a *neuro*divergent brain, pathways can get crossed, signals can be too strong, or something else may be happening that science hasn't yet identified. What we can do is turn off flickering lights or allow someone to wear a hat with a brim when inside to block triggering light. And as Temple Grandin explains, even looking at a board or screen across the room can be a problem because the lettering appears fuzzy or squiggly. She suggests that wearing tinted glasses could be a simple fix for such an individual.[43]

A Lack of Inner Sight: An interesting side note on the sense of sight is a condition in which someone lacks the ability to visualize or to imagine something in their mind.[44] Aphantasia (from the Greek word for without imagination) is not described as a clinical disorder. Yet it affects up to three percent of the population. One study found that people with aphantasia reported more autistic traits than a control group.[45]

Touch: Hyperesthesia is a condition causing extreme sensitivity to touch, pain, pressure, or thermal sensations. It has been identified as a neurological condition, which means neurons are not working in a typical way. In autism, there may be a variation in how touch stimuli are processed in the neocortex. Someone with ADHD may have a strong aversion to certain textures or material. Tags in clothing is an example. Keep in your teacher's mind that touch and textures are a consideration.

The Hidden Senses of the Vestibular and the Proprioceptive Systems: There are various sensory processing disorders that involve the vestibular and proprioceptive systems. It is not within the scope of this book to discuss each one, but two examples can provide a sense of some disorders. Sensory-based motor disorder (SBMD) creates challenges in coordinated movement and in planning sequences of movement. If you are thinking this could greatly limit a child's ability to play (ride a bike or kick a ball), you are correct. Sensory discrimination disorder (SDD) diminishes the ability to distinguish similar sensations. For example, a child may be unable to identify an object by touch alone.[46] Lucy Jane Miller, PhD, OTR, provides an informative and engaging book, *Sensational Kids: Hope and Help for Children with Sensory Processing Disorder (SPD)* (2014), on this important topic.[47]

What Do You Need to Know?

We are back to the starting point of this chapter. You do not have to understand the brain science of neurodivergent processing to create a program sensitive to these children's processing considerations. Neuroscience has provided much accessible information to use as a general guide. For example, knowing there is science to explain why a messy room or messy art table can cause some children to fixate on what is askew or jumbled is enough. Knowing there is science to explain why someone can have a compulsion about controlling personal space or using a certain mat is enough. All you need to know is that these conditions can cause someone to become anxious or avoidant, to fixate, or to disengage. Again, look to the underlying causes, which are based in body physiology. It's not a typical class.

Barry Prizant, PhD, has devoted his professional life to studying and supporting those affected by autism, including families and professionals. His book, *Uniquely Human*, is an accessible and gentle guide to understanding autism. His central message speaks to challenges of those with differing needs and autism: The behaviors aren't random, deviant, or bizarre.

> It's not an illness, but a different way of being human ... What's most vital, for parents, professionals, and society as a whole, is to work to understand them and then to change what *we* do ... in other words the best way to help ... is to change ourselves, our attitudes, our behavior, and the types of support we provide (p. 4).[48]

With specific planning and teaching considerations, we can use Dr. Prizant's compassionate insights to shape what and how we teach. A planning checklist is available to support your efforts to set everyone (including yourself) up for success (see SR-C.7). The first consideration is why building a sense (*feeling*) of safety and creating a positive learning environment are central to this art and yoga program.

CHAPTER 4

Yoga as a Healing Tool

The central theme of this book is the central theme of the GreenTREE Yoga®️ Approach: Building a sense (*feeling*) of safety needs to guide every part of every program. As you read this chapter, notice the role of safety in the benefits from breathwork, movement, and learning.

Movement

There are physical, emotional, and mental benefits to moving. And practicing yoga is a way for someone to move. But first, keep in your teacher's mind that how much someone moves is not the important point. We can take some advice from the brilliant physicist turned body worker, Moshé Feldenkrais, PhD, who said there is "not a right way to move, there is a better way to move."[1] So, as we teach, the goal is to support children in finding that better way to move. And please also keep in mind that a better way to move is based on how it *feels* to that child, not how it looks to any adult in the room. A note from the renowned author and yogi T. K. V. Desikachar underscores this key point in any yoga program: "Much more important than these outer manifestations is the way we *feel* the postures and the breath."[2] Quite simply, doing yoga is about how it feels, not how it looks.

Body Awareness: One major benefit to moving is that it can help build body awareness. As discussed, body awareness is critical to building self-regulation skills. To review, *feeling* you are getting upset needs to happen before you can do something to calm yourself. Let's take that idea and add that small movements build body awareness. Dr. Feldenkrais developed an Awareness Through Movement (ATM) program. He believed that awareness comes through small movements made slowly. Quite simply, "Movement is the basis of awareness."[3]

The relevant general physical benefits of moving are increased flexibility, improved strength of bones and muscles, increased health of joints, reduced pain, and improved posture, stability, and balance. Another benefit to movement is improved immune function.[4][5][6]

Regulating Emotions: In addition to the physical benefits, movement has emotional benefits as well. Science continues to show that moving and exercising create physiological changes in the body that can lower stress levels and improve mood.[7][8][9] One example is that when muscles move, a biomolecule called atrial natriuretic peptide (ANP) is released, which can interrupt the stress cycle.[10] The fact that moving your body can lower stress levels might have led to the thought: "Aha, lower stress levels mean a child is better able to learn." You would be correct. If you would like more science and some heartening stories filled with possibilities for using movement to heal both the body and brain, you might enjoy *Spark: The Revolutionary New Science of Exercise and the Brain* (2008/2013) by John Ratey, MD. He presents the science down to the molecular level of how movement and exercise can help many conditions, including anxiety, depression, addiction, and even ADHD. You may have noticed these conditions have a self-regulation element.

Changing the Brain: Now let's consider what moving does for the brain and mental function. First, movement supports cellular repair processes, as discussed in *Exercised: Why Something We Never Evolved to Do Is Healthy and Rewarding* (2021) by the evolutionary biologist Daniel E. Lieberman, PhD.[11] In *Spark*, Dr. Ratey says, "... exercise has a profound impact on cognitive abilities and mental health."[12] While this art and yoga program is not aerobic exercise, it is stretching and movement. It may also build the strength, balance, and coordination skills that support children in doing more active things. As discussed, the brain can rewire or change (neuroplasticity). The relevant note is in a book by Michael Merzenich, PhD, a leading expert in the field of neuroplasticity. In *Soft-Wired: How the New Science of Brain Plasticity Can Change Your Life*, he identifies simple ways to support brain plasticity. Perhaps as you read these quotes, envision a child practicing some fun yoga poses. Dr. Merzenich says, "As you move, focus on the feeling of the flow of that movement."[13] He adds another idea: "Move with your whole body, you have a flexible core and a spine, use them."[14] Dr. Merzenich is a world-renowned neuroscientist and does not refer specifically to yoga. He also says that we should explore new ways to move. Quite simply, we should provide Show, Don't Tell opportunities, to move with a flow, to move the whole body, and to move in a playful way. To me these ideas on how movement can rewire the brain sound like the yoga component in this book. After all, yoga is both an art and an empirical science based on thousands of years of observation.

Of course, how much movement and how much exercise someone needs to reap all these benefits remains the topic of much discussion and research. But what seems clear is that (unless told otherwise by a medical provider) moving is better than not moving.

The Breath

The Heart of any Practice: Breathwork (practicing how you breathe) is not a yoga add-on that might be included if someone leaves enough time. As the renowned yoga teacher and author T. K. V. Desikachar noted, "The breath should be your teacher."[15] Managing one's breath can be a primary stress management tool for everyone, which can make it part of your self-care too. And remember, the brain is most able to change (rewire) in children. Don't miss opportunities to teach children these simple self-regulation skills.

Huffing and Puffing: Please be sensitive to the physiological fact that all breathwork is not the same. As with anything you introduce into your trauma-informed space, be informed. Some breaths can be highly agitating: for example, breathing that causes sudden shifts in affect (feeling) states. Tummo or Wim Hof breathing are examples. The loud sounds of someone huffing or panting on the next mat (Bellows Breathing or Ujjayi Breathing) can also be quite triggering (see the information on misophonia in the 'Sensory Processing Disorders' section in Chapter 3: Differing Abilities and Neurodiversity). One of the main takeaways from James Nestor's engaging book, *Breath: The New Science of a Lost Art* (2020), is that breathwork is a powerful tool in affect regulation.[16] His engaging melding of personal experiences, science, and cultural history is inspiring. But, like any tool, breathwork can be used and misused. Be mindful of what noises you introduce, and that includes breathing. Again, and again, be informed.

My Big Mistake: This breathwork section is to inform and to inspire your teaching, parenting, or counseling. Yet someone does not need to know all the science to benefit from breathwork. Breathing is a natural thing, and most children find their way. I was working with an extremely bright 12-year-old boy. Because I shared too much breath information, he lost his natural connection to his breath. He became so agitated that he began holding his breath. I noted *my* big mistake and never repeated it. I then suggested he simply put one or both hands over his heart for 3 breaths: "Feel the breath in ... Feel the breath out." (*Say 3 times slowly.*)

Just Breathe: Now let's look at the physiology behind, "A few deep breaths out *can* be calming," and "A few deep breaths in *can* perk you up." If you would like to experience the science of managing your breath, look at the left side of Figure 4.1.

If it's comfortable, begin to practice some longer breaths in. Your lungs are expanding as the dome-shaped diaphragm muscle drops. If your body didn't have self-regulation loops, you might start to feel faint. But as you breathe, a signal is being sent via the vagus nerve from the heart to the brainstem. The signal is that your heart rate is slowing, so your blood pressure is dropping. So, the return message from the brainstem to the heart, again via the vagus nerve, makes the heart beat faster. Now your blood pressure goes up, and you are mentally and physically prepared for what you need to do. This science is why longer breaths in *can* be energizing.

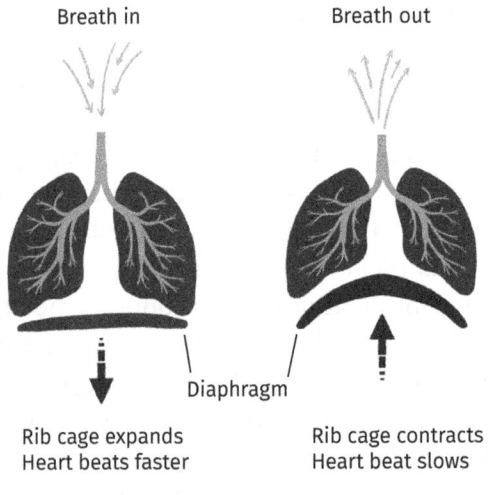

FIGURE 4.1: THE SCIENCE OF BREATHING

Just Breathe, Take 2: Well, what if you don't want your heart to beat faster and your blood pressure to go up? Again, to experience another way to manage your breath, look at the right side of Figure 4.1. When you are ready, notice your next breath in. Then, practice a long, slow breath out. Do you notice how the diaphragm muscle has returned to its original shape, much like a rubber band? Another signal is being sent via the vagus nerve from the heart to the brainstem. You don't need as much oxygen now. So, the return message slows the heart rate, which lowers blood pressure and also lowers muscle tension. This breath science is why longer breaths out *can* reduce heart rate and lower blood pressure.

A Note: It's important to know that either breathing pattern can increase levels of agitation and anxiety for some. Trauma-informed teaching is not to tell someone how to breathe or how it will make them feel. Your job is as a guide.

It's a Matched Set: In my experience, pairing simple breathwork with one simple physical movement gets the job done. That job is to teach body awareness in a way that supports someone in noticing their breath. Again, this section was included to support *your* understanding of the science of managing your breath. It is not helpful to overload children with breath facts. As simple as that.

Fun and Play

Play and the Periaqueductal Gray: Why is a section on fun and play in the science chapter? Because there is science that shows the biological benefits of playing. These benefits include: 1) feeling safe enough to try new things; 2) thinking (cognition) about things in a new way; 3) lowering stress levels; and 4) improving social skills. The foundational research of Jaak Panksepp, PhD, identified seven primary emotions wired into the mammalian brain for survival.[17] Play is one of the seven. Playing, in both children and adults, stimulates the brainstem area called the periaqueductal gray (PAG), which secretes endogenous (natural) opioids. These natural opioids create a feeling of safety. Feeling safe allows time for the thinking part of the brain (prefrontal cortex) to explore different scenarios and to become more plastic, that is, more able to rewire.[18]

Stephen Porges writes that play first provides an opportunity to experience a bit of anxiety (trying something new). Then playing with others can activate the social engagement system, which supports someone self-regulating back to feeling safe.[19] There is more research being done on the benefits of play (having fun) for children with autism and other conditions.[20] The main message from science is that your class will have many more benefits if it is ... fun and playful.

Birthday Parties: Keep in your teacher's mind that fun and playful for children with differing needs and learning styles is not the same fun and playful for a typical group. Bouncing into class as the latest action hero, playing lively, loud music, and encouraging children to run around the room is for *neuro*typical birthday parties. It is not for these groups. But as you will notice in later chapters, there are still many ways to make the class fun and playful within the parameters of safety, empowerment, and simplicity.

Learning

Practice: Understanding how someone learns can make us better teachers. The body physiology of learning is that as we practice something, either thinking about it or doing it, neurons fire faster so signals get sent faster. This faster signaling means we improve our performance. And stronger connections (more neurons firing together) are made as we learn a new way of doing or responding to something. *Practice* is the first part of *learning*. Think about learning to tie a shoe or ride a bike, or changing how you react to something. If you looked at your brain scan, you would see certain parts of your brain lighting up, identifying how the signals are traveling in different parts of your brain. The information first gets encoded in the hippocampus and then is sent to other parts of the brain for storage. With over 90 billion neurons in the brain alone, there are many neurons and many pathways.[21] But, of course, it's not that simple.

Pay Attention: Neuroscience tells us something parents and teachers already know. To learn, you need to be paying attention. Daniel Siegel, MD, says, "Attention is the scalpel of neuroplasticity."[22] What does that mean? Quite simply, it means that paying attention sets the stage for learning. Neurotransmitters needed to encode new memories (learning) and to rewire the brain (neuroplasticity) are secreted when we pay attention. Acetylcholine and then dopamine set the learning process in motion. It's ... body physiology.

Let's build on that idea of attention. Consider how well you learn when you are very stressed or upset. One reason that stress affects learning is body physiology. The body gets flooded with stress hormones (adrenaline and cortisol are some). In the short term, these stress hormones are important in getting you ready for action with the fight-or-flight response so you can move to safety or mount an attack. While you might remember where the dangerous snake lives (stress hormones encode this memory), you are not thinking through choices and consequences (stress hormones inhibit thinking). And studies continue to show that long-term stress can inhibit the formation of new memories (learning) and over time can kill neurons in the part of the brain that first encodes memories, the hippocampus.[23 24 25]

A Quick Review

How safe someone feels affects their ability to pay attention. The key to helping someone practice and then learn new ways of responding to stress is to first lower their stress levels. The tools of movement, breathwork, and having fun come to mind. Throughout this book, the intention is to *practice* and then to *learn* more adaptive ways of self-regulating. The approach is to use the body, the mind, and the breath. Now, let's look at what a simple art project and a simple yoga practice can bring to this noble teaching intention.

PART II

GETTING STARTED

A report in *The American Journal of Occupational Therapy* may be inspiring. Parents who had brought their neurodivergent children to occupational therapists completed a survey. Parents hoped to build these skill areas: 1) social participation and acceptance; 2) self-regulation; and 3) self-esteem and confidence.[1] You will notice that this art and yoga program is designed to address each of these points. For themselves, the parents wanted two things: 1) strategies to help their children succeed; and 2) what Diana Henry calls a toolbox to get them through the day.[2]

These written comments from parents who participated in this art and yoga six-week program may inspire you to continue exploring this program.

"Loved the art, best projects and she has them all hanging up and loves to show them to people."

"Thank you so much for this. We have worked on a lot of the breathing exercises. H. likes the one where he does a fist and breathes out. He has a really difficult time with body awareness and motor planning, so this had been a really great (and fun!) addition to our therapies. I also love that there is a social component to it as well. Thank you so much again!"

"S. does enjoy the yoga class, and to my big surprise even art!!!"

"H. loves the yoga and it's really a great tool for both of my boys. We love this class. A great program!"

"I was so excited too when P. finally participated ... The little things are great!"

"We loved it. Just the right amount of yoga and fun. Looking forward to more!"

"One of my sons benefited from the motor planning and another greatly benefited from the breath."

"Really appreciated the continued improvement of core balance in a non-therapy setting."

"Following direction and imitating was huge for K. To follow direction and imitate with her body was great to see—she used to not even look at the person or have any interest in trying just up until about 6 months ago."

What Was Helpful About the Program

- Having a schedule to follow.

- Having the yoga mats for sense of space.

- Including the kids for suggestions and choices.

- The art projects always had a lot of different sensory components.

- Learning relaxation techniques, especially ones to use at home and in school.

This art and yoga program also provides parents with hands-on, easy-to-use materials to use at home with their children to reinforce what is practiced in the classes. In addition, the program provides parents with yoga breaks for managing their personal stress both at home and at work. Several formats make the short breaks easy to use: audio (MP3s), video (MP4s), and handouts (see SR-D and SR-E). Let's look at how to get your program started.

CHAPTER 5

Preparations

Scheduling Your Programs

There are various ways to schedule a program. Each has its own considerations.

You Initiate Contact: You can make initial contact with schools, yoga studios, clinical groups, or community centers. Sending your descriptive flyer and a follow-up phone call can serve as a good introduction (see SR-F).

You Respond to a Request: A school, yoga studio, clinical group, or community center may contact you. Some basic considerations can help you plan a successful program.

1. **Schools, Yoga Studios, and Fitness or Community Centers** may want programs after school, on weekends, or during a summer camp. It may be one class or a series. Programs open to the public can attract diverse groups, which means there are two planning considerations. The first is limiting the number of people attending. The second is planning what to do if a child becomes disruptive or dysregulated. Taking the time to consider your classroom management plan is key to a successful class (see the 'Classroom Management' section in Chapter 6: Building Safety). This plan can prevent a complete breakdown of your otherwise well-planned class.

2. **Clinical Settings** have different programming considerations. You may be working with one clinician in a private setting, which simplifies program development. But when working with an organization or facility, there are other considerations.

- **Yoga Will Help.** This following situation is not uncommon but can be avoided with coordinated planning. A well-intended staff member has been told that yoga is a good thing for these children. They leave the teacher alone on the assumption that yoga cures all. So, before teaching, it is important that you meet with staff to clarify your role as a yoga teacher. This meeting will establish that a staff person needs to be present at all times. You should not be expected to manage issues outside of teaching yoga. It is also unfair to others in the group to expect a yoga teacher to meet those needs.

- **Teaching Points.** Before I had developed this program (which means before I had given it much thought), I was invited to teach at a camp for children and teens. Each week would be different ages and different physical, emotional, and mental challenges, which I was not told ahead of time. On my first day, I arrived as the counselors helped three children from wheelchairs to lying on yoga mats. We were not doing a floor practice. How many teaching points can you identify? Let me make my list. I didn't know I could ask about the composition and ages of each group ahead of time. I didn't know to let the counselors know ahead of time what we would be doing. I didn't know to let the staff know ahead of time how they could support my program. I didn't know ahead of time that the way to answer this teaching invitation was not simply, "Sure, I would love to." Did you notice that each point has *ahead of time* in it? I will say that the classes went well, meaning we had fun. But with more communication in the planning stages and with ideas on how to extend the program (for students, parents, and staff), I feel confident it could have had a stronger and a more lasting positive impact.

Your Social Connection: Establish a way to contact parents and staff before, during, and after the art and yoga program. It also allows for feedback.

- **Introduction.** As appropriate, contacting parents/caregivers/clinicians before the first class presents a well-planned program (see SR-F.2). Include a picture of the activity board so the children know what to expect. They will see the familiar chart next to you when they come into the room. Include a Shanti the Monkey coloring sheet for the first day's pose. Children might want to color Shanti at home, to think of a name for the pose, and to bring the colored sheet to class. Note what snack (water and fresh fruit) will be served and that parents are welcome to bring their own snacks if that is a better fit for their child.

- **Two Days Before Each Class.** At the end of each class, note that you will provide the new coloring sheet two days before the next class. But always offer the sheets at that time, as it may reduce parental stress. Set up for success.

Organizing the Yoga

Choosing Poses and Breathwork: Based on the needs of your group, carefully plan the poses to include in the Shanti flip chart sequence as outlined in Table 13.1 (see Chapter 13: Class Format). This program can be adapted for a variety of developmental ages. Two age groupings that have worked well in my programs are 3–5-year-olds (30/40-minute program) and 6 years plus (1-hour program). Part V: Teaching the Art and Yoga Curriculum provides information on: 1) teaching breathwork and the poses; 2) full teaching scripts; and 3) clipboard notes.

It's About Time: Planning the yoga poses and breathwork to fit your time frame is one key to success. It is not helpful to say, "Oh, sorry, we are out of time and won't get to do this part!" I have heard that said. Then the schedule, which is on the activity board for all to see, has been disrupted. Children's expectations have not been met.

The Power of the Clipboard: Clipboard notes are provided to support your planning process (see SR-C.3). You can note: 1) the specific times for each component; and 2) the phrases you want to use. Keeping the clipboard by your mat (or chair) gives two important messages to both the children and the adults: You are organized, and you care about timing your program well. That sentence is worth rereading. Be nice to yourself and use the teaching support materials to feel confident, so *you* can have ... fun.

It's Still About Time: Perhaps your style is to arrive at class 5 minutes early, toting only your yoga mat and a smile. As some say, "This is not that." As you read suggestions on organizing the yoga and then the art, please make a strong mental note that you need time before class to set up the room and art table. If the room is in use until 11:00, plan your class start time accordingly. The person assisting you should be available to help you set up more quickly. If you haven't planned enough time, you haven't set everyone (including yourself) up for success.

Organizing the Art

For a smile and a sense of possibilities, before you read this section, perhaps first look at the photographs of the art projects and some children who created them (see SR-A).

Materials: Each art project in Chapter 15: Six Art Projects has a list of materials. The intention is to choose materials based on sensory stimulation considerations. Let's review these important considerations to use as a general guide.

- **Sight.** Colorful choices can be positive. Prepare enough materials, as some children may want to do the entire project using one or two colors. Some will avoid certain colors. Including shiny finishes (some foil papers) can bring diversity and opportunities for choice. A visit to a craft store can expand your offerings. I discovered felt with some shiny imprinted designs. Triangles cut from pieces of old yoga mats also provide a different look and feel.

- **Touch.** There are many ways to introduce tactile sensory experiences through your choice of materials. For example, triangles cut from smooth shiny (foil) paper, yoga mats, construction paper, and felt (textured and regular) each provide different sensations. Sticky glue or sandpaper can be a negative tactile experience.

- **Smell.** Let the sniff test be your guide. Glues can be smelly. Wash pieces of old mats (unscented detergent) before cutting them for the triangle art projects.

- **Hearing.** Why is the sense of hearing in the art section? In the tree pose project (see the 'Class 3: Tree Pose' section in Chapter 15: Six Art Projects), the suggestion is to crumple small pieces of pre-cut tissue paper to glue to the tree template. It's both tactile and auditory. Knowing that I am craft-challenged, someone shared a cute dog puppet made from a paper bag with pompom ears and a felt tongue. I thanked her, but can you *sense* why it wasn't a good idea? Paper bags make a lot of noise. Very small pieces of tissue paper do not.

- **Taste.** It can be a fun note to include a variety of tree nuts and fruits for the snack on the tree pose day. Coconuts, peaches, oranges, walnuts, and almonds are some examples. It can be interesting to compare the textures of whole fruits or the shells of various nuts. The suggestion is to have the eating samples already prepared, along with the option of a whole fruit available to pass around. Be mindful of nut allergies: A rule of thumb is always to avoid peanuts.

Organizing the Art Materials: Presentation is a key part of creating a successful art experience. Here are two reasons to give careful thought to how you present the art materials, and you may think of more. Looking for patterns is one way some children make sense of their world. A messy art table can cause anxiety, or a child may fixate on the disorder. Another reason is an orderly table supports different processing styles. Simple choices support safety and empowerment.

- **Separate Containers.** The suggestion is to minimize disorder by putting the materials in separate, similar containers. Clear, small plastic trays with dividers can be useful. Markers or crayons can be sorted by color.

- **Sticky Stuff.** Pouring some school glue (no odor) onto a small white paper plate before class starts allows the glue to be ready for the art project. Popsicle sticks can be used to apply glue. For projects that need stronger glues (those with beads or pipe cleaners), an adult can oversee a hot glue gun away from the art table.

The Art Table: You may have guessed that considering the art table can build a stronger program.

- **Art Table Surface.** You may not know what table will be available when you arrive, so come prepared with a cover. I once bought a cheerful flowered tablecloth. When I got home, I realized the colorful patterns would be distracting. Using a light-colored paper (butcher block) or a plain, plastic tablecloth can solve the problem of covering scratches or stains. It is a sensory thing. It is not a little thing.

- **The Art Table, Take 1.** Consider walking into a room. The first thing you see is a table piled with art materials. Give yourself a moment to envision several trays of colorful triangles in all sizes and materials mixed together. There is one large bin of types and colors of markers and scissors in the middle. During yoga, you might be distracted by or fixate on the table, trying to make sense of the jumble. Then it's art time. Everyone sits around the table that has crumbs on it. It has marks and dried glue from other days. The teacher talks on and on while passing out things.

- **The Art Table, Take 2.** Now consider walking into that room. The art table has covered bins on it. At art project time, you sit around the table while the teacher unpacks the bins trying to decide where to put things. She talks about a project you don't have in front of you. You might see how these two scenarios do not create a positive start.

- **The Art Table, Take 3.** Last one to consider. You walk into the room. The art table is off to the side, neatly laid out with orderly, sorted materials. The table has a clean, smooth, white covering. Each space has a white paper plate. The teacher greets you and says, "Find your yoga spot. The art table is over there, all set for our project today." The teacher then points to the activity board. "As you can see, we will do our art project after we do our Hello Song and some yoga." Order has been restored. It is not a small point.

Organizing How You Teach Art: You may have the room organized. You may have the art materials organized. There is one more piece to organize. You can organize how and what you teach.

- **Activity Board.** One example is that you point to the activity board as you say, "We did the Hello Song, we did yoga, and now it's time for art. We can go to the art table and have our snack there. Then we are set up to do our art project." In my experience, using the activity board as a touchpoint throughout the class is important, as it eases the stress of transitions.

- **Many Rockets.** You hold up one finished project. "Today's art project goes with rocket pose. I made this rocket. Let's see how many different rockets we can make today." It's important to have an easy-to-make template so everyone feels successful. But it's as important to allow for creative expression. My son, a talented artist and neurodivergent thinker, helped his art-challenged mom create some fun projects from the templates.

- **Sharing Facts.** It is both important and easy to keep children engaged. Asking who has a rocket fact to share (or anything relevant to that day's pose) acknowledges strengths and individual interests. It is also a fun way to build social connections. Barry Prizant, PhD, tells how the late Clara Claiborne Park, an English professor and one founder of the National Society for Autistic Children, answered a question about her daughter's obsessions. She said they had always considered them *enthusiasms*. Dr. Prizant devotes a chapter to the importance of *enthusiasms*, that is, the strategy of focusing on a particular topic as a way of gaining a sense of control, predictability, and security in a world that can seem out of control.[1]

  You can include questions in the art time, and you will find cues throughout the scripts that celebrate *enthusiasms*. "Who knows an interesting fact about cobras?" It is yet another way to adapt your program to the interests and abilities of your groups.

- **Personal Space.** Children choose their materials from your orderly containers. "We have colored paper for the covering and wings. We also have some stickers and beads." Children (parents or volunteers may help) can place the chosen materials on the white paper plate that marks their personal space around the art table.

- **Different Styles.** "I have envelopes so you can take your supplies and finish your project at home." One 10-year-old took extra triangle pieces home to finish his creation. You can see the photo his mom showed me of the beautiful, completed project laid out on a deep purple piece of cloth (see SR-A). It's also important to have extra materials and scissors/ markers available so adding to the template is possible. Eagles have feet. My template did not. One boy calmly solved the problem by cutting out legs and feet to complete his eagle (see SR-A).

- **Extra Templates.** One autistic 9-year-old had a vision for his triangle project. He started one template after another, a total of four. He was not being difficult. It was not a behavioral issue. He was being creative. He could see the stack of triangle templates in the middle of the table, so he felt comfortable asking for another one. Set up for success.

- **Extra Shanti Coloring Sheets.** Having extra coloring sheets and crayons available for children who come early or who forgot theirs is both welcoming and inclusive.

To Recap: Why is it helpful to review some suggestions for being a well-organized teacher? Being predictable and consistent is critically important to working successfully with children with differing learning styles and physical needs.

- **Clipboard.** The clipboard notes can help you to organize and plan the class, to keep track of time, and to note the phrases you want to include. Plan your program so it fits into the allotted time for each activity.

- **It's About Time.** Plan enough time to get your room set up for both the art and the yoga activities. If you cannot visit the room before the first class, ask a staff person to give you information on the space. They may be able to do some of the setup before you arrive. For example, they could move extra furniture out of the room or make sure you have a table with enough chairs to go around that table.

- **Art.** Three considerations create a stronger program. The first is to carefully choose the materials. The second is to take care in how materials are presented. Both steps should reflect a strong awareness of sensory stimulation considerations and physical and mental challenges. Finally, the third consideration is how you organize your teaching of the art project.

PART III

BUILDING SAFETY, SUPPORTING EMPOWERMENT, AND MAINTAINING SIMPLICITY

The GreenTREE Yoga® Approach is based on three key objectives to improve physical, emotional, and mental health. Let's look at how this art and yoga program addresses these objectives: building safety, supporting empowerment, and maintaining simplicity. It's not possible to clearly separate them. Yet it is this overlap that creates a strong program as the intertwining ideas reinforce one another. What does that mean? Well, when you teach to empower, it builds a child's sense (*feeling*) of safety, as they feel stronger and more in control (an overlap of safety and empowerment). When you teach simple yoga poses using simple language, you make *feelings* of empowerment more accessible for children (an overlap of simplicity, empowerment, and safety). You may note more points of interplay and synergy as you read the next three chapters. Therefore, let's organize our discussion around these intertwining objectives of safety, empowerment, and simplicity.

CHAPTER 6

Building Safety

To review, as Stephen Porges, PhD, explains, when someone feels stressed, anxious, or unsafe, their physical and emotional resources are diverted to mounting and maintaining a defensive strategy.[1] Or quite simply, because someone does not feel safe, they are distracted and anxious. They are not set to learn or to heal or to have fun. It is body physiology. Therefore, again and again, it makes sense that the first consideration in working with children with differing abilities and learning styles is to build a sense of safety. How can you use a body-based yoga practice to build a sense (*feeling*) of safety? Well, saying, "You are safe in this room," doesn't get it done. Telling someone they are safe uses the verbal part of the brain, so it may not be processed quickly or easily. Keep in mind that feelings of being unsafe or stressed are often feelings held in the body and processed on a visceral or subconscious (without words) level.[2] Let's look at ways to build this feeling of safety so the many benefits of art and yoga can then be experienced.

The Room

Give yourself a moment to visualize a room in which you want to share art and yoga. Okay, how many variables come to mind? Well, location, room size, floor covering, lighting, windows, doors, furniture, and cabinets come to my mind. Did you consider the people in the room? There may be children, parents, caregivers, staff, or volunteers. Did you remember that you are also in the room? And there are your supplies and materials: yoga mats or carpet squares, snacks, and art supplies. What else? There may be sounds from outside the room, heating vents, or yet-to-be-heard sounds. Did you think about the smells in the room? So, a room is quite a bit more than four walls and a table.

Islands of Safety: The good news is you do not need a perfect space in which to share your program. With consideration of a variety of factors, you can control what you can (and you may be surprised at how many things you can control) and work with the rest. Building a safe space can give children what Peter Levine, PhD, calls an island of safety.[3] From there, even if stressful or triggering things happen, children may be better able to manage their responses. This program's body-based, trauma-informed yoga practice becomes an opportunity to expand someone's island of safety. They can *practice* and then *learn* new coping strategies.

Your Yoga Space: Using yoga mats or carpet squares can create a sense of personal boundaries and personal space. Children can use these visual and physical cues (mat, carpet square, or chair) to orient and to ground in their yoga space. How you use these props is another way to use this important teaching guide: Show, Don't Tell. It is another way to build a feeling of safety.

Yes, It's Your Yoga Space: Partner poses can intrude on that sense of safe personal space. Partner poses can also cause confusion, anxiety, noise, and discomfort. Therefore, they are not included in this program. Parents or caregivers may find ways to connect with their child as you teach, but the suggestion is *not* to cue partner poses. Of course, teachers and clinicians familiar with their groups may have different protocols for touch and for partner poses. I will note that in one third-grade classroom, two students often helped a boy with clear physical challenges. So, without my prompting, each stood by his wheelchair as they all happily held hands and practiced their own pose variations. Three big smiles told me his choice to have partners was a positive part of his practice. I will also note that for the first two classes, he parked his wheelchair in the back of the room and simply watched. The third class he wheeled up to me and announced, "I am Joseph. I am here to do yoga." And he stayed right in front of me with his friends for every class after that.

Where's the Teacher? Moving around the room can create anxiety, as the children may not know where you are or what you are going to do. This program's intention is to focus on practicing yoga, not to create distractions from a teacher on the move. Strong startle responses are not uncommon. Staying on your mat can build a sense of safety in the room. It means you are not touching students either. Again, the exception would be for those working with groups or individuals for whom touch is a part of the typical teaching protocol.

Classroom Management

Most would agree that a primary intention for managing any classroom is to build a sense of safety. As discussed again, and then again, it is simple body physiology that without feeling a personal sense of safety, someone's abilities to learn and to self-regulate can be greatly compromised. Yet, managing a classroom for children with differing needs is not the same as managing a classroom for a neurotypical group.

What Am I Managing? Your job is to manage the art and yoga program. And your job is to manage that program in a way that considers the laundry list of needs identified by science and common sense. This book provides a useful and accessible guide to that important list. What *isn't* on that list is how you should manage a child's meltdown or state of dysregulation. Why? Not because you are unfeeling or not up to the task. Again, the simple fact is that your job is to teach a well-designed program.

Blue Shorts on Tuesday: While you can design a program to address general physical, emotional, and mental challenges of your group, you cannot know each child's concerns and triggers. Those triggers can vary not only among the children but with each child, depending on the day. It could be that an autistic child sits on their mat and notices their mismatched socks. Perhaps the correct Tuesday shorts are in the wash so the day is already off to a shaky start. It may be some new behavior or sensitivity being exhibited. A child may be tired, as sleep issues are common. So even a small group in a quiet space is still too much stimulus. None of these concerns is something you should have to address. Why? Because trying to solve dysregulation problems takes you away from managing the carefully planned art and yoga program and from meeting the needs of the group.

Not So Fast: However, that is not the last word. If a meltdown goes unattended, you have shown poor classroom management skills. But how can that be? Because it's your program. There are two key things you should have done in advance of teaching.

- **One.** You need to make it clear what activities will be included and what will be happening in the room. Examples include noting the group size, the activities, and the suggested ability level. It then is up to the parent, guardian, or clinician to determine if your program is a good fit (see sample flyer in Appendix E). Communication becomes an important planning tool. For example, a parent may let you know that their child needs to wear a baseball cap inside (light sensitivity). A parent may tell you that the child needs to see the door or must always be in the same spot each class. A classroom teacher may let you know it's a mixed-needs group—and that's all the information they have (which was said to me in a class of 25 children).

- **Two.** You need to clearly identify the person responsible for assisting any dysregulated child. Again, and again, you are teaching art and yoga. Part of your program requirement may be that a parent attends with each child. In a clinical or classroom setting, it may be that several staff members (aides, volunteers, teachers, or clinicians) attend. You may be a clinician sharing some art and yoga, but the considerations remain the same. Other adults need to be present. These ideas put a different spin on classroom management, not surprisingly, because these groups are different. With some advanced classroom management planning, you can set yourself, the children, and the adults in the room up for a successful experience.

A Note: A quick way to get the room quiet is to put your hands over your heart (visual cue) and simply say, "Okay, everyone. Listen for your breath. That's right, listen for your breath." In 2 breaths the room is usually quiet.

Sensory Considerations

What We See: Visual cues are important safety cues for sighted individuals. This fact means visual cues can be another tool in this important teaching guide: Show, Don't Tell.

- **Limiting Stimulation.** The suggestion is to limit each class to five or six parent/caregiver and child pairs, with no more than 12 people per class. A small class size means you can better manage the environment. Limiting stimulation also applies to yoga mats: Avoid wild colors or bold patterns. Choose mats of the same color or as few colors as possible.

- **Clutter.** Sometimes the room is a lovely, clean, quiet spot. Sometimes it is not. The suggestion is to do what you can. For example, close cabinets doors. Push extra furniture neatly to the side. Avoid stacking things in random piles.

- **Arranging the Room.** Sometimes you have options for arranging your space. Sometimes you do not. Limiting sensory stimulation is a useful guide. My preference is a semicircle of mats, carpet squares, or chairs around me. But what will children see behind you? Cluttered counters? Windows looking onto a busy hall? The art table? One room in which I taught had windows looking to the community indoor pool. I placed the mats so that I looked out that window toward the pool. The children looked toward a row of cabinets I had closed and counters I had cleared. Another space in which I taught was a large gym. I put my mat against one wall to create a small semicircle, with the children looking at me. Again, with a bit of time and thought, you can minimize distractions.

- **More Arranging.** Suggestions on how to arrange the art table are outlined in the 'Organizing the Art' section of Chapter 5: Preparations. It's a primary consideration in managing visual stimuli.

What We Hear: As discussed in the 'Sensory Processing Disorders' section in Chapter 3: Differing Abilities and Neurodiversity, low tones can signal danger and be upsetting. And some children have auditory considerations in which they hear mostly low tones. Others are sensitive to any noises (see the information on misophonia in the 'Sensory Processing Disorders' section in Chapter 3: Differing Abilities and Neurodiversity). How you use sounds is another way to build safety.

- **Music.** The suggestion is not to play music. Children can then notice their breath and notice bodily sensations without distractions. While music therapy has many strong benefits, you can't know what music may distract or upset someone. An exception is if you are working with a group or individual for whom soft music is a part of the typical teaching or clinical protocol. One of our teachers taught private classes to an autistic 18-year-old. The parents shared that listening to nursery rhymes calmed her. This talented teacher used that music to frame her teaching.

- **Roars and Barks and Hisses.** "If you like, softly meow once as we do cat pose." This quiet sound cue can keep children engaged, prevent auditory overload, and help to build self-regulation skills. For example, while doing downdog you all can bark quietly once. While doing cat or cow pose, meowing or mooing quietly once keeps it interactive and fun.

- **Other Sounds.** Even jangling bracelets can create distractions and unease. And again, be aware of potential art materials (using paper bags, ripping any type of paper) and yoga accessories (chimes, sound bowls) that could create auditory issues.

What We Smell: Smells can trigger someone with sensory issues or in trauma recovery. Consider these ideas for managing the smells in your space.

- **Mats.** Outgassing from new mats can cause headaches. Unroll the mats several days before use, preferably outside. New mats may also feel slippery from chemicals. It may be necessary to wash them first. Used or donated mats should be washed as well. Do a test run, but many mats wash well in hot water, unscented detergent, and unscented bleach. Mats can be line dried. If you use a spray cleaner or wipe down the mats with a cleaning solution, be aware of residual scents or slippery substances. Dryer fabric softeners can be heavily scented, not a good look on a yoga mat.

- **Scents.** Avoid perfumes, scented hand creams, candles (scents and smoke), strongly scented flowers (lilacs), smelly glues, or incense. Each can add triggering smells to the space.

What We Taste: While research is ongoing as to the effects of sugars, additives, and preservatives on children, many parents appreciate snacks that steer clear of processed foods and sugary drinks. If you bring snacks to share (to build social connection at the art table before art), water and pieces of fresh fruit, served with plastic spoons in small bowls, are usually welcomed by all.

Teaching Intentions

How do we set children with different learning styles up for successful learning? Matching your teaching intentions to your actions provides a strong foundation. Let's consider four teaching intentions to provide that foundation: 1) self-regulation; 2) body awareness; 3) predictable activities; and 4) clear boundaries.

Self-Regulation, Practice, and Learning: A child can practice breathwork (self-regulation skills) with you. Providing that opportunity makes a strong teaching intention. But again, keep in your teacher's mind that *practicing* and *learning* are two different things. To review, practicing is the first step. Practicing Feel the Breath may help a child to *feel* calmer and safer, which then sets them up to learn. You have successfully taught self-regulation skills if *practicing* leads to *learning*. Does a child want to teach the Open and Close Breath (Fist Breathing) or Feel the Breath (see Chapter 14: Scripts for the Yoga Practice) to their cat (a 5-year-old did), their sister, or a friend on the playground (yes, a teacher shared that a little girl from our class did)? Later, someone may notice, "Oh, I am feeling mad. But I can do the Open and Close breath." Or "I feel sad. Rocket pose makes me smile. I will teach it to my brother." One mom told me that her 11-year-old autistic son told his brother, "I am really mad. I am going outside to breathe." As simple as that.

Body Awareness: Let's look at building body awareness (interoception) as a key step in learning. A sense of your body, that is, feeling your toes press on the floor or feeling you are becoming upset, is the first step to learning to manage stress or frustration. It's body physiology for everyone. A body-based yoga practice teaches body awareness through simple cues to notice bodily sensations and to practice simple body movements. "When you feel your leg muscles ... when you feel your leg muscles, wiggle your fingers." Or "If you like, look at your fingers. Then stretch your fingers as wide as is comfortable today." Tables 12.1, 12.2, and 12.3 (Chapter 12: Teaching Intentions) provide additional ideas on this important teaching guide: Show, Don't Tell. While the reasons may differ, each of the following three areas can be challenging.

1. **Grounding.** If someone is grounded, it means they are fully present. Being fully present is not yoga-speak but rather an important part of both *practicing* and then *learning*. Being present means you are physically, emotionally, and mentally aware that it is now. You are not distracted by anxiety, stuck in the past, or worrying about the future. Again, to rewire the brain (learn) in a more adaptive way, you need to be paying attention. A connection to the present using physical sensations and breath awareness creates that feeling of being grounded. Very simply, you pay attention to what's happening in your body right now.

   However, saying, "Okay, you need to get grounded," can be frustrating and confusing for anyone, as it gives no specifics on how to do it. This art and yoga program uses clear, simple cues for body and breath awareness as a tool to help someone *feel* grounded. One example is: "When you *feel* your big breath in, press down on your toes ..." Feeling your breath in or noticing you are pressing down on your toes can only happen in the present. Show, Don't Tell.

   As Barry Prizant, PhD, notes in *Uniquely Human*, activities in which an autistic person might engage (rocking, flapping, stimming—repetitive motions) are often not defects but strategies to feel grounded when the sensory environment is overwhelming or they feel anxious or bored.[4]

2. **Proprioception and periphery.** Weaving references to *feeling* bodily sensations in the hands and feet (or arms and legs) or to *looking* at the hands and feet while moving or holding a pose does several important things. 1) It strengthens *feelings* of internal awareness, which as discussed, is key in the ability to self-regulate. 2) It supports improving proprioception, or the sense of where one's body is in space and how it is moving. 3) It can develop and refine personal boundaries. A teenage girl with clear mental challenges was lying on her mat as I was teaching. She blurted out, "Where do I end? Where do I end?"

3. **Twists.** Children can benefit as their arms and legs cross the midline of the body. This physical action of a gentle twist helps develop a sense of where they are in space. The gentle physical action can also calm the nervous system, as the body posture is not signaling fight-or-flight.

Predictable Yoga Sequences and Activities: Having a predictable and consistent sequence to class activities can allay the anxiety and discomfort of the unknown. It can create smoother times of transitions. You can avoid putting a child in the position of having to wonder, "What will happen next? I don't like new things. What if I don't know what to do? What if I don't like it?" Consider how these three points can strengthen your program.

1. **Stay Connected.** As noted in Chapter 5: Preparations, contacting parents or staff can provide a predictable structure and set up smoother transitions throughout the class. You can include the coloring sheet class and a picture of the activity board for parents to share. Also included could be the audio (MP3) of the short break you will be practicing that day, so the parents have it for the coming week (see SR-D). In addition, this connection allows for parents to ask questions or send comments. A follow-up point of contact is included so you can assess your program. It lets you know what is working and what needs improving.

2. **Activity Board.** The activity board, as discussed in Chapter 13: Class Format, provides simple opportunities both to engage the children and to reinforce the class structure. You can ease the stress of transitions by continually referring to the activity board always located next to you. After each section is complete, first point to the card indicating what you have completed and then point to the card for what comes next. Pairing auditory and visual cues supports differing learning styles and reinforces that the class is predictable.

3. **Shanti the Monkey Flip Chart.** Keeping the same order of Shanti the Monkey poses in the flip chart is another simple way to show that your class is both predictable and consistent (see Chapter 15: Six Art Projects). Using the flip chart along with the simple question, "Who remembers what pose Shanti the Monkey practices next?" is engaging and serves as simple visual and simple auditory cues. Usually someone remembers, but if not, you could say, "Well, I remember. It's cobra pose!"

A Note: Photo stands from a craft shop can sit on the floor and hold the activity board and the flip chart—one on either side of you.

Boundaries: A boundary means something has a beginning and an end.

Maintaining boundaries is an important teaching intention. Two suggested boundaries, written in the scripts to follow, can build a sense of safety in your room. Always begin with the child, which means the child's sense of personal space. A strong start is providing each child with a mat, a carpet square, or a chair. Then, to give more definition to the physical personal space, each yoga practice begins with a few stretches and fingertip presses to mark that yoga space—over your head, to the sides, and to the back. "That is your yoga space today. We all stay in our own yoga space." You have given visual, auditory, and tactile cues to define personal space. You have let everyone, both children and adults, know this yoga class isn't going to be chaotic, with others running around and stepping on each other's mats. You have let everyone know you aren't going to be wandering around, putting your hands on someone, or startling them from behind. That one simple sentence said it all. It's as simple as that.

Now, what's the boundary in these cues? "Let's practice 3 breaths," or "If you like, practice 2 breaths as we move in mountain pose." Time has become the boundary. Cueing the number of times establishes a simple, clear, safe boundary. You avoid the distraction of someone thinking, "How long are we doing this? Do I even want to be doing this? Is she done yet?" Instead, someone might think, "Oh, today I want to practice 2 breaths."

The Value of Interactive Teaching

Social Engagement Revisited: This section is entitled the value of interactive teaching to highlight this important teaching opportunity. As the teacher, you do most of the talking in the room. Children may look toward or at you or be listening as you offer suggestions. Therefore, you become a key component in how children gauge safety: the voices and facial expressions of others. Stephen Porges' ideas on the social engagement system are relevant here. Quite simply, your calm voice and your friendly face can soothe an anxious or oppositional child and even a stressed parent.

The Value of Your Signals: Your voice and your facial expressions become important tools to use for at least three reasons.

1. Fewer brain signals may be processed in these children. So make sure those that are processed are helpful. Being consistent in all you say and all you do can accomplish this intention.

2. Too many brain signals may be processed, so children can be highly sensitive to sounds. You want the sounds of your voice to strengthen, not detract from, your program. Simple ideas on how you can fine-tune your sound are in Chapter 10: Ways to Practice How You Teach.

3. These children benefit from practicing reading social cues. So the positive social experiences you create can also help these children rewire their brains in more adaptive ways. Again, this rewiring happens as someone thinks about or physically does something.

Processing Social Cues: Certainly, much has been written about the challenges neurodivergent children can have in processing social cues. One example is gaze aversion in some autistic children. Gaze aversion may be a way of self-soothing by preventing overstimulation in one part of the brain. It's not consciously rude behavior. To repeat, as Barry Prizant, PhD, notes, many of these autistic behaviors (rocking, flapping, gaze aversion, stimming) are strategies to self-regulate. But gaze aversion can greatly impair someone's ability to connect with others. It is why autism programs may have classes in social skills in which children practice interacting with others and practice socially acceptable responses.

The Value of Interaction in Real Time: This art and yoga curriculum was developed to be taught in person. While a recorded class can provide consistency, teaching that is live (in the room or remotely) can be interactive and dynamic. One example is pointing to the Shanti flip chart and asking who knows what pose comes next. Sometimes the most unlikely person will happily say, "Cat pose!" A recorded class denies the children, the parents, clinicians, and you those social connections created through sharing a fun experience. But there are more reasons to keep your teaching interactive.

The Value of Adapting for Your Group: As noted before, collaborating with parents and clinicians to develop an appropriate program is important. What you bring to that collaboration is your ability to adapt this program. Each child can be so different, which makes each group different. Becoming familiar with this art and yoga curriculum is a starting point. While the basic teaching principles remain the same, teaching in person (again, in the room or remotely) allows you to continue adjusting how you teach. For example, as children become more familiar with the yoga sequences, the class pacing may change. Offering classes of various lengths of time can address varying attention and energy levels. You can also adjust the number of poses included (making sure the order stays the same) as needed. More able children need pose variations to keep them engaged. This process of adapting your program also keeps you engaged as you plan and teach.

The Value of Fun and Play: Science supporting the positive role of fun and play is discussed in Chapter 4: Yoga as a Healing Tool. It is considered again in this section because some children's yoga programs seem to lack a sense of play. One static yoga pose after another, taught in a perfunctory manner, lacks the fun factor. What delighted me about Louise Goldberg's book, *Yoga Therapy for Children with Autism and Special Needs* (2013), was her clear acknowledgement that yoga needs to be fun. Children with differing abilities and learning styles would probably appreciate more fun in their days. Quite simply, when doing something in a playful manner without any pressure to perform, things open up. What things? 1) As discussed, a place that *feels* safe enough to try something new opens up. 2) A place that *feels* safe enough to play with an unknown outcome opens up. 3) An opportunity to explore a new physical sensation or a new breath or a new way of handling an emotion opens up. So, yoga done as a chore because an adult says it's good for you or done as one static pose after another, even if taught with the best of intentions, can miss a valuable opportunity to empower and to add cheer to a child's day ... and to yours.

CHAPTER 7

Supporting Empowerment

As you read this chapter on supporting empowerment, you may notice the overlapping trauma-informed objectives of safety, empowerment, and simplicity. As previously noted, so much of each day can feel out of control or too challenging to children with differing abilities and learning styles. For more able children (ages 8 years and up), Temple Grandin's 2023 book, *Different Kinds of Minds: A Guide to Your Brain*, empowers through information as she clearly and accessibly explains the challenges and strengths of neurodivergent brains. The book can be a key resource for empowering children and the adults in their lives. Now, let's consider the various ways this art and yoga program can empower children using the mind, the body, and the breath.

The Power of Choice

By Design: This program is designed to continually offer ways to practice making small personal choices. Yes, making choices can be practiced. A child enters the room and chooses their spot. They may have chosen to bring a mat from home. They may choose to sit on their mat and not do any yoga. They may choose to join the yoga practice later. A child may choose to put their mat against a back wall and observe for some time. A child may choose to sit quietly on their mat with their parent who is doing the yoga. In one class, a 7-year-old boy simply sat next to his mother on their shared mat for three classes. Then he joined in. An 8-year-old boy sat to the side for two classes, observing before he joined us. Did I confuse everyone by explaining all the options? I did not. The simple greeting of, "Welcome, pick out your mat," was enough. Did I mention that sitting next to your mom or dad was fine? I did not. I taught the class. My voice and facial expressions showed I was not upset by children making their own choices. As simple as that.

　More Choices: Why is there such stress on choice as an empowering tool? Again, making choices is something to be practiced. And there are children for whom a lack of choice or a perception of being told what to do can trigger oppositional or avoidant behavior. So, yes, this program stresses the importance of choice through both your choice of language and your actions. A child's opportunity to practice making choices continues with choosing how to do a pose today. A suggestion is to remember: More is not better, more is confusing. Offering two choices can be empowering; offering more can be distracting and upsetting. A simple choice should set everyone up for success.

Using invitation language can be empowering. This suggestion does not mean saying, "I invite you to ..." To my ear that means someone needs your permission or your invitation to do something. "I invite you to ..." is an example of well-intended yoga-speak that misses the mark. Well, then, what could you say? I learned two phrases from David Emerson: "When you are ready ..." and "If you like ..."[1] Each phrase is also grounding, as someone could think, "Am I ready?" and "Do I want to?" Both need to be considered in the present. Both are empowering. Both are simple. Other opportunities to practice making choices during the art project time will be discussed.

The Power of Positive Phrasing, Pacing, and Pauses

Great Job! Your word choice can provide acknowledgement and support empowering a child. Or it can do the opposite. "Good job, Maria!" could make someone else wonder if they did a good job or why you didn't notice them. "Sasha, it looks as though your tree pose makes you feel strong today," is without judgment. If you like, read this next cue aloud and notice how it makes you *feel*. "If you *can't* put your hand on the floor, *just* put it on your knee in triangle pose." Now read this cue aloud: "Today it may be more comfortable to put your hand above your knee as we create a triangle pose." Same pose using simple, empowering phrasing instead of negative wording. Imagine starting your art project and hearing, "If you *can't* finish your project, you can *just* take some materials home." Now imagine the teacher saying, "If *you would like* to finish your project at home, I have these envelopes so it's easy to take your materials home." Same information, but with simple empowering phrasing: *can't finish* becomes *would like to finish*. And the word *just*, which only serves to minimize, is not used.

The Art of the Pause: Part of your plan should include how quickly you speak and how you use the mighty pause. If working with differing abilities and learning styles is new to you, it may take some practice. As an example, after I recorded the yoga breaks, they were reviewed by someone who had devoted 30 years of her professional life to working with autistic children. Each time she said the same thing. "Yael, I love the content and your voice. But it's too fast." After four recordings, I finally got it right. (Thank you, Shelley!) During a live class (in-person or remote), the art of the pause is gauging the correct pace by watching the children as they process what you say and find their own ways to practice. If you ask a question and someone wants to answer, make sure you give them enough time. The practice for you is to assess how long to wait for someone to answer before you move on. You want to find that spot in which they have enough time to process the idea but not so much time they feel they have failed. I learned this art from watching Dawn Young teach in her warm and supportive and empowering way.

The Power of Strength: Core and Balance

Another way to support empowerment is building physical strength. These children often have extra challenges with body awareness, body control, and body strength. The yoga poses in this program are chosen to address these challenges. Such poses as triangle, rocket, eagle, and tree can build core strength and balance. The poses are taught so that everyone is set up for success and can develop some sense of mastery. Feeling physically stronger can build self-confidence and a sense of control. Using a wall or a chair while doing the poses can increase a sense of being grounded.

The Power of Normalizing

To normalize means to make something more typical or normal so it's less out of sync with the rest of the world. Many of these children go through their days feeling they are lacking, deficient, or abnormal. Quite simply, they don't fit in. This program is a wonderful opportunity to normalize what each child brings to the class—their physical, emotional, and mental abilities. You can help to normalize what they *are* able to do in a few simple ways.

Inclusivity: One way to normalize is to be inclusive. Consider a group in which one child is sitting while others are standing. "When you are ready, come back to standing tall." Who did you leave out? Who may feel unseen and as though they don't belong? It is simple to say, "When you are ready, come back to sitting or to standing tall." I like to say the seated cue first because ... well, why not? Another idea is to use the same inclusive cue even if everyone is standing. Two reasons support saying, "When you are ready, come back to sitting or to standing tall." One is the message to all (children and adults) that it's fine to sit or to stand at any time. You have no expectations. The second reason is it becomes a habit for you to teach with inclusive language: *practice* leads to *learning* for you too.

There is yet another way to build inclusivity into your language. "Stretch all ten toes," or "Stretch all ten fingers," assumes what? I learned I needed a better cue when working with veterans and, as I said that cue, noticed someone with three fingers on one hand. It reminded me that my cousin has six toes on one foot. "Stretch all ten toes," can become: "Stretch all your toes." "Stretch ten fingers wide," can become: "Stretch all your fingers wide." As simple as that. These are some ideas, and as you give it some well-deserved thought, more may occur to you.

Let's Practice: Another way to normalize abilities is by using the word practice. In yoga, we are always practicing. There is no end point or finish line. "*Take* 3 breaths," can become: "Let's *practice* 3 breaths." "*Do* cobra 2 times," can become: "Let's *practice* cobra 2 times." Why the change? The words *do* and *take* are both directive. Let's *practice* has a decidedly different tone.

You may have noted that such language is another simple way to prevent some oppositional or avoidant triggers. The cue: "The suggestion is to practice 2 breaths," can add more choice to your teaching.

Big Dogs, Little Dogs: Using the word practice also acknowledges that children may be doing different things. Consider the message in the simple opening cue: "There are many kinds of dogs, and there are many ways to practice the downdog pose." Or "Trees come in all shapes and sizes." Or "There are many kinds of rockets." It's a message to the adults in the room that you are not looking for the children to do specific things. It's an important and often welcome message.

A Day to Feel Strong: Consider the simple suggestion: "Find a way to practice peaceful warrior that makes you feel strong today." You have set the stage for variations, as children may feel comfortable exploring ways to move that feel strong today. Giving specific cues that externalize the pose (put your hand here, make sure your foot is there …) works against children feeling safe and comfortable exploring different ways to move. Quite simply, it takes the fun out of it. Not done yet.

Let Me Help You: I have been in classes in which a well-intended parent or caregiver continually moves, repositions, and monitors how a child is doing a pose. Again, the above cues can send a clear signal to that well-intended adult: If the child is enjoying it, they are doing it right. Adult intervention is not needed or expected. You may have noted that this approach could lower anxiety levels in the parents as well. Feeling judged and being corrected because you (or your child) did something *wrong* works against everything in this program: safety, empowerment, and simplicity. Of course, exceptions are if a health care provider assists a child so they can experience the connection between words and movement or if it's part of other health care protocols.

One of my favorite photographs is of a class practicing downdog. One child is sitting by his mom. Another child has one hand and the opposite leg lifted as he smiles grandly. Another child is in a classic downdog pose wagging his pretend tail. Another is in puppy pose. Well, you get the idea. (Many thanks to Dawn Young for creating that class.) There are many kinds of dogs in the world. I am sharing some of my ideas based on my teaching experiences. And again, finding your own ways to normalize variations can keep you mentally engaged as you develop and teach your programs.

Art: To review, another opportunity to normalize personal choices and abilities is during the art project. "Let's see how many different kinds of rockets we can make." Or "These envelopes are to take home if you want to finish your project later."

CHAPTER 8

Maintaining Simplicity

As you read this chapter, you can notice how the third component of the GreenTREE Yoga® Approach (simplicity) intertwines with the other two components (safety and empowerment). To maintain means to keep or to provide. To maintain something in a program means it is a thread throughout that program. As discussed in Chapter 3: Differing Abilities and Neurodiversity, these children can have a host of information processing challenges or other physical, emotional, or mental challenges. Keeping it simple means there is a better chance they can understand and then find their own way of doing what you are suggesting. You may also not know everyone's challenges. Therefore, your strongest teaching strategy is to keep every aspect of your program simple: everything you plan and teach and everything you say and do. I taught simple yoga breaks in classrooms with over 20 children with diverse abilities. I played audio breaks as I did them with the children. I was able to leave the audio breaks for the teachers to do with the children later (see SR-D). It was a success because we had fun, there were lots of smiles, and they enjoyed the Shanti coloring sheet. As simple as that.

There are three ways to keep it simple: 1) use simple language; 2) offer simple yoga (simple breathwork and simple poses); and 3) pair simple auditory cues with simple visual cues. Let's look at each way.

Simple Language

Language is a key communication tool. Language comes in a variety of forms. If you ask someone a question, how many ways might they relay their answer? Perhaps they speak. They might write something. They could shrug or move toward you. They may make an expressive face or sign something. So language can include verbal language, written language, sign language, and body language. Let's talk about verbal language. It's especially important in working with children who may not be adept at reading facial and social cues or at processing words. There are many ways to keep your language simple.

Consistent Language: Quite simply, use the same language in your cues. "Lift one arm toward the ceiling ... Then raise your hand as high as you can," uses different words for the same move. It is not wrong, but it gives someone's brain more information to process. It can distract from finding and then *feeling* the stretch.

No, Your Other Left: Children can be distracted, confused, or embarrassed when trying to find their left side. "When you are ready, lift your left arm to the side or over your head," can become: "We always do both sides. When you are ready, lift *one* arm to the side or over your head." It's as simple as that. "When you are ready, lift your *other* arm ..." Again, a child may already have enough frustration in their day. Simplicity sets everyone up for ... success.

Literal Language: Using imagery or flowery language is not wrong. But it can greatly complicate someone's ability to process what you are saying. "Stretch toward the ceiling," is literal. "Grow your tall branches toward the sunny sky," can muddle understanding of what should have been a simple suggestion. Again, and again, it is helpful to remember that brain processing circuits are highly variable. A good filter is to ask yourself, "Is this action literally possible to do? Can I really reach the clouds? Can I float like a balloon? Do my feet reach into the earth like roots? Can I take off into space? Do I have a tail to wag?" You can still be fun. It's as simple as saying, "We don't have tails, but if you feel like being silly today, pretend to wag your tail like a happy puppy." A dad told me that his little boy answered his grandma's comment, "You are the apple of my eye," by saying, "But Grandma, an apple wouldn't fit in your eye." He was distracted from her loving comment by the image of an apple not fitting in her eye. Being literal can mean being a more effective communicator.

Table 8.1: Figurative and Literal Language

Figurative language (imagery)	Literal language (realistic)
"Press your hand *into* the floor." You can't press a hand into the floor.	"Feel your hands press *on* the chair (or floor)." Someone can *feel* their hands pressing.
"Stretch your arms to the sky. You can almost touch the clouds." You can't almost touch the clouds.	"Stretch toward the ceiling." Someone can see/feel their arms stretching. A sighted child can also see the ceiling.
"Imagine you are a willow tree blowing in the wind." A child is not a tree. A child is a child.	"Stand in a way that makes you feel strong today." Someone can explore ways to *feel* strong in a pose.

Simple Repetition: Simply repeating a cue accomplishes several things. "When you are ready, put one or both hands over your heart … Put one or both hands over your heart." This simple repetition provides the same information and allows more opportunity to process what's being said. It then allows the time for someone to find their way of doing what has been suggested. And there is more. Your voice is still there as a thread to safety, instead of leaving dead air. But using different words or throwing in an irrelevant comment tangles that thread to safety.

The Sounds of Language: As discussed in 'Polyvagal Theory, Social Engagement, and Self-Regulation' in Chapter 2: Stress, Polyvagal Theory, and Self-Regulation, the intonations and pacing of your words can have a strong effect both on someone's sense of safety and on someone's ability to understand your words. We come back, again and again, to the fact that auditory concerns need to be considered. So, keep the sounds of your voice … simple. Okay, but what does that mean?

- **Fast or Slow … High or Low.** What are some examples of your vocal sounds? Wild swings in your tone or using a sing-song voice can prove annoying and sound condescending to everyone in the room. There is more to keeping your sound simple. How quickly or how slowly you speak (pacing) is also important. If you speak too quickly with many words and ideas, it can be complicated for someone to process. Keeping your voice well modulated is another way to keep it simple. Speaking softly and then getting louder to make a point can confuse the meaning and diminish the sense of safety in the room. Keep it simple by using your own voice. Be confident that as you practice for teaching groups with differing learning styles and abilities, you will sharpen your overall communication skills.

- **The Message Riding Along with Your Words.** Okay, now what does that mean? When you speak, you are giving more information than your words. Do you sound nervous? Do you sound rushed? Do you sound bored or confused? If your words sound confident and like you are having fun, it's a stronger program. So, the question becomes: Have you ever listened to yourself teach? You may not know that you rush or you put in extra words, because that's how you have always taught. There is an easy solution, one which will make your program stronger and more useful. You can listen to how you sound. Four simple steps to practice the sounds of your teaching are given in Chapter 10: Ways to Practice How You Teach.

Simple Yoga: Poses and Breathwork

Set Up for Success: As noted again, and again, for many children with differing abilities and learning styles, each day is an unending series of challenging or overwhelming tasks. A sure measure of a successful program for children with a variety of physical, emotional, and mental challenges is that they *feel* they had fun. This program's breathwork and poses were selected because they are fun and can be taught in a simple way. There are no complicated movements or triggering breathing patterns. The poses build strength, balance, body awareness, and confidence. The poses are offered as simple stretches with room to grow. The breathwork is easy to practice because it's paired with a simple movement and doesn't introduce triggering sounds or create sudden affect (feeling) changes.

Adapting Challenges: Planning two challenges or pose variations can add texture to your classes and keep more able groups engaged. But in some groups, it can be empowering to name something as a challenge that you know everyone can do. "If today is a challenge day for you, wiggle all your toes ... wiggle all your toes." This simple cue sets everyone up for success. Yet sometimes offering a more challenging variation can allow a child to feel a sense of growth. The suggestion is to demonstrate the challenge but then to stay in the basic, simpler version of the pose.

Simple Verbal Instructions and Visual Cues

Avoid the Laundry List: One instruction at a time keeps it simple. "Lift one arm out to the side or toward the ceiling, spread your fingers wide, then wiggle your fingers," can become: "When you are ready, lift one arm out to the side or over your head ... (pause as you slowly provide the visual cue, while children find their own way) ... If you like, spread your fingers wide ... (pause) ... Today you may want to wiggle your fingers." How long do you pause? That's an important question based on your awareness of different processing styles. Look to your group as you find your rhythm of cueing. The suggestion is to allow time for children to: 1) process what you are suggesting; 2) find their own way to do what you are suggesting; and 3) notice how it feels. What may be new to you is finding your rhythm as you teach based on closely monitoring the needs of your group.

Pairing Visual and Auditory Cues: How you choose to use visual and auditory cues takes on added importance in these groups. Some children may be visual learners, which is why the Shanti the Monkey flip chart, the activity board, and an in-person teacher consistently doing the poses from the same spot in the room are important. Some children process auditory cues more easily, which is why clear, simple language is important. Some children may go back and forth. Therefore, it's strong teaching to pair both simple cueing options, as one can reinforce and simplify understanding of the other.

PART IV

SET *YOURSELF* UP FOR SUCCESS

This section is about you. We talked about setting your students, clients, and children up for success. It's well worth noting that setting yourself up for success is also an important component to a strong program. Why? Bringing your best self to the game means you can be a better teacher and find more enjoyment in the process. Let's consider how you can make that happen.

CHAPTER 9

Self-Care: Taking Care of You

If you *sound* unsure, exhausted, rushed, bored, or stressed as you teach, it will probably come across in your voice and facial expressions. If you spend all your energy taking care of others, and if you consider taking care of you to be selfish or unnecessary, the suggestion is to keep reading.

Being Practical

When I teach workshops on self-care, I offer that taking care of yourself is not being selfish, it is being practical. If you get sick or experience any physical, emotional, or mental challenges from stress, you may not be able to provide the care and patient understanding you would like. You, in fact, may become someone who needs to ask others for help.

Let's look at what self-care means and why it's important. Let's look at some simple, quick, and free ways you can practice simple breathing and stretching breaks to manage your stress both at home and at work. As discussed in Chapter 2: Stress, Polyvagal Theory, and Self-Regulation, we have stress feedback loops that should naturally lower stress levels when the stress has passed. But experiencing high levels of stress most of the time is chronic stress. Years ago, the advice was to change jobs or to stop complaining. You may not be able or even want to change jobs (home or work). Fortunately, a lot has changed since the days of those unhelpful pieces of advice.

The Cost of Caring: Compassion fatigue is a term coined in 1992 by Carla Johnson, a nurse who described how some nurses stopped paying attention to their emotions when working with very sick patients.[1] A few years later, Charles Figley, PhD, called compassion fatigue the cost of caring.[2] The word compassion comes from the Latin words *pati* (to suffer) and *com* (with). So, compassion fatigue is the physical, emotional, or mental fatigue that can come from suffering with someone. Let's stay with this idea.

Does This Happen to You? We have talked about how a teaching intention can improve body awareness and self-regulation skills. We have discussed how this program can help children notice when they are *feeling* upset and can give them some self-regulation tools both to *practice* and to *learn*. And this approach can also provide you with many benefits. A chronic stress scenario could be that you don't even notice your feelings anymore. That's a missed opportunity to practice some simple, quick, and free ways to lower personal stress levels. Another scenario is that you notice but ignore your feelings because you are too busy caring for others. Perhaps you are too tired to deal with it. These responses are not uncommon and are very understandable. But let's consider another way.

Reframe to Empower

There is an alternate plan to believing that you need to toughen up or that you should not take time for your problems. Instead, consider your responses to stress as important pieces of information about you.

The First Step: As Jack Kornfield, PhD, notes in his book, *The Wise Heart* (2008), noticing is the first step to change.[3] Noticing is being mindful or aware that something is happening now. Noticing gives you the opportunity to decide what to do next. It can be useful and empowering to pull an insight from Milton Erickson, MD, to complement this mindfulness practice of noticing how you feel.

The Power of Reframing: Dr. Erickson wrote that you could reframe that feeling or observation.[4] Quite simply, you could consider it in a new way. Instead of staying in the stress loop of feeling overwhelmed and out of control, you could consider it as an empowering opportunity to practice a self-regulation technique you already are teaching the children. "I feel myself getting angry." Or "I feel myself getting overwhelmed." Or "I am exhausted." You could choose to reframe these feelings as opportunities. "Oh, I could practice the Anytime, Anywhere Breath with long breaths out to lower my blood pressure." Or "Three shoulder rolls back would feel good right now." Or "I can take some deep breaths in as I practice the Finger Stretch Breath to perk up." How you choose to respond to your feelings is exactly that—your choice.

Short Breaks for You

To empower yourself, consider these simple, quick, and free breathwork and simple stretching breaks. These trauma-informed resources are available as MP3s, MP4s, and handouts (see SR-E). The suggestion is to practice one short break and notice how it makes you *feel*. As with children, first we *practice*, then we *learn*. Quite simply, it can become a habit to notice a stressful feeling and then quickly practice that break you've experienced to be a useful way to change how you are feeling both at home and at work.

- **Break 1:** Shoulder Rolls/Feel the Breath (2:28)

- **Break 2:** Tip-to-Toe Stretch/Shoulder Rolls/Finger Stretch Breath (5:21)

- **Break 3:** The Kitchen Stretch: Find a New Stretch/Kitchen Stretch/ Shoulder Rolls/Finger Stretch Breath (6:58)

- **Break 4:** Tip-to-Toe Stretch/Finger Stretch Breath (3:26)

- **Break 5:** Seated Cat/Cow/Finger Press Breath (2:56)

- **Break 6:** The Anytime, Anywhere Breath (2:57)

Your Planning Checklist

Why is there a planning checklist in the self-care section? Arriving to teach with all the materials you need, a strong plan, and enough time to set up is a good way to set yourself up for success.

YOUR PLANNING CHECKLIST
The Room

☐ Visit or call for information on the room setup

☐ Allow enough time/people to set up the room

☐ Know your options for managing children who may need to leave the class

Shanti the Monkey

☐ Shanti the Monkey: extra coloring sheets with crayons for before class

☐ and the new sheets for the next class (option for parents)

☐ Shanti the Monkey flip chart (updated for each class) with stand (craft store)

☐ Activity board (5 cards) on foam core board with a stand (craft store)

Art

☐ Materials for that day's art project

☐ Extra envelopes to take materials home

☐ Table covering (clean and plain)

Yoga

☐ Yoga poses and breathwork plan

☐ Clean mats (not smelly or slippery) or carpet squares

☐ Complete your clipboard notes with: 1) times for each activity; 2) phrases to use in this class; and 3) the MP3 break for yoga part 2

Yoga Breaks

☐ One breathing break (MP3) to practice during yoga part 2 (include in the pre-class contact to the parents/staff with that day's coloring sheet)

CHAPTER 10

Ways to Practice How You Teach

Why is practicing how you teach an important part of your self-care? Because being more confident in your teaching can lower your stress levels and set you up to have fun. After all, laughing is a long, slow breath out, which can lower heart rate, lower blood pressure, and lower muscle tension. This chapter and the supplemental materials include steps to practice, a follow-up questionnaire to fine-tune your teaching, a planning checklist, and clipboard notes.

Your Sound

Let's start with how you sound. I offer this personal example. When I first started recording audio yoga breaks, the person recording asked if I wanted to hear how I sounded. I said no. I even remember saying, "I sound like I sound." A bit later, he politely asked again, and I again said no. Then I started doing my own recording and editing, so I had to listen to how I sounded. I listened so carefully that when I was teaching an in-person class and my voice cracked, in my mind, I saw the audio program mistake. I even remember saying the word again correctly as I taught. I found it amusing how far I had come. I suggest there is a middle ground between, "I sound like I sound," and editing in your mind as you teach a class.

Four Simple Steps

These two breathing breaks and one yoga pose are from the full scripts in Chapter 14: Scripts for the Yoga Practice. Many easy-to-use, free phone and computer apps are available to download for recording audio.

Step 1: Record the audio for the script Feel the Breath (later in this chapter). Practice the break as you record it.

Step 2: Listen to your recording 3 times. It's easier to listen for one point at a time. Perhaps jot down some notes as you listen.

1. **Tone:** Play it once. Notice how you sound. Do you sound rushed? Is it a sing-song voice? Do you sound bored? I notice that I sound bored when I am tired.

2. **Pacing:** Play it again. Notice your pacing. Too fast or too slow? Do you allow enough time for someone: 1) to process what you are suggesting; 2) to find their own way to do what you are suggesting; and 3) to notice how it feels? Or did you leave long empty pauses in which someone might feel adrift?

3. **Word Choice:** Play it again. Notice if you put in extra words or if you changed the script as you recorded it. Remember, keeping consistent, predictable, and simple wording is key. A GreenTREE Yoga® guide is: More is not better, more is confusing.

Step 3: Make the Changes from your notes as you record it again.

1. **Changes:** Play it again. Notice if you made your changes.

2. **Practice:** Play it again. This time practice with your recording.

Step 4: Invite someone to do it with you.

1. **Teamwork:** Play the break as you do it together.

2. **More Teamwork:** Ask for feedback. Sometimes providing a short form with specific questions can give you valuable information as you fine-tune your style (see SR-C.9). You may find either written or verbal responses useful.

Continue to Practice How You Teach: If you found this exercise helpful, notice if there are fewer edits as you continue to practice.

1. **Repeat** steps 1–4 as you record the It's a Wrap Breath.

2. **Repeat** steps 1–4 as you record tree pose.

Practice Scripts

These scripts offer a solid place from which to start your program. Again, the suggestion is first to practice as they are written. You may find you like the rhythm and simplicity. Or you may want to make certain changes to fit your personality. But whatever changes you make, the suggestion is to keep your wording simple, literal, and body based.

Feel the Breath

1. "When you are ready, gently press one shoulder back ... Then press the other shoulder back.

2. Put one or both hands over your heart ... Put one or both hands over your heart.

3. Let's practice Feel the Breath 2 (or 3) times.

   Feel the breath in ... Feel the breath out. (*Say 2 or 3 times slowly.*)

4. When you are ready, look at one hand. If you like, gently *wiggle* the fingers on that hand or shake that hand ... Then look at your other hand. Gently *wiggle* the fingers on that hand or shake that hand. Now look at both your hands. How still would you like to hold your hands?"

It's a Wrap Breath

1. "If you feel like being silly, wiggle your arms all around ... wiggle your arms all around.

   Side 1: When you are ready, create an arm wrap. We always do both sides.

   Side 2: When you are ready, put your other elbow on top and create another arm wrap.

   Let's practice 2 It's a Wrap Breaths.

   As YOU breathe in, press down on your hands ... As YOU breathe out, release the press.

   (*Say 2 times slowly.*)

2. **Side 1:** If you feel like being silly again, stretch your arms wide and wiggle your fingers.

   Side 2: If you still feel like being silly, stretch your arms wide and do something that *feels* silly today.

3. When you are ready, look at one hand. If you like, gently *move* the fingers on that hand or shake that hand ... Then look at your other hand. Gently *move* the fingers on that hand or shake that hand. How still would you like to hold your hands?"

Variation: "Gently *move* the fingers on one hand ... gently *wiggle* the fingers on the other hand." (*For more able groups.*)

Tree Pose

1. "Shanti the Monkey is practicing tree pose. Trees come in all shapes and sizes. When you are ready, sit or stand tall. Set yourself up so you *feel* strong today.

2. We always do both sides. If you like, wave one hand. Can you tap your leg 3 times with that hand? Tap ... tap ... tap. When you are ready, turn that knee open like Shanti the Monkey. You can keep your toes on the ground today. If today is a challenge day, you can press your foot against the standing leg. Maybe today you *feel* strong with your hand on the chair.

3. Do you feel like being silly?

4. **Side 1:** You can pretend your arms are tree branches moving in the wind. Is it a strong wind today? That's silly.

   Side 2: Can you move around in tree pose until you smile? Now, that's silly.

   Side 1: When you are ready, come back to sitting or standing tall. Today you might want to shake one leg 3 times. Shake ... shake ... shake. Then shake out the other leg. Shake ... shake ... shake. Now, how still would you like your legs to be?

   Let's practice tree pose on the other side. (*Repeat above.*)

   Side 2: When you are ready, come back to sitting or standing tall. Who knows a tree that is very strong? (*See enthusiasms p. 58.*)

5. If you like, gently press one shoulder back ... Then gently press the other shoulder back. Let's practice the Finger Stretch Breath 2 times.

6. As YOU breathe in, *stretch* your fingers ... As YOU breathe out, release the *stretch*. (*Say 2 times slowly.*)

7. When you are ready, look at one hand. If you like, gently *move* the fingers on that hand or shake that hand ... Then look at your other hand. Gently *move* the fingers on that hand or shake that hand. How still would you like to hold your hands today?

(You may have a child who is amused by not holding their hands still, a wonderful practice of making choices and body awareness. You did ask them ...)

Who remembers what pose Shanti the Monkey practices next?" *(Flip to next card on chart.)*

FOLLOW-UP QUESTIONNAIRE FOR YOUR RECORDED TEACHING
(Available in SR-C.9 to print)

I am looking for ways to make the breaks more useful to children and families, so please check 1–5, with 1 being not at all and 5 being very much. Thanks for your feedback!

	(not at all)			(very much)	
	1	2	3	4	5
I feel better after the break.					
Use fewer words.					
It was too fast for me.					
It was too slow for me.					
I would like to practice it again later.					
Record it again so we can give it another try.					

Any other comments? (Thank you!)

. . . .

. . . .

. . . .

. . . .

. . . .

. . . .

. . . .

TEACHING THE ART AND YOGA CURRICULUM

Part V covers both the why and the how of teaching this art and yoga curriculum. It makes sense to start with the *why*. Why do art, yoga poses, and breathwork have benefits? Then from this base of understanding, we can move on to the *how*. How can you teach these easy-to-use ideas and bring benefits to both children and their parents?

CHAPTER 11

Benefits of Art and Yoga and Breathwork

Benefits of Art

Social Connection: The art project and the snack are times of easy interaction for both children and adults (parents, teachers, clinicians, and volunteers). It's an important part of the class. Parents have noted their surprise at children talking about computer games, giving each other ideas on the projects, and laughing. This time can also provide social support for the parents, who can feel isolated by their children's challenges. Another benefit is that children like to display their projects at home. This wonderful visual cue may prompt them to share their art with someone, to practice a yoga break, or to remind them that they are part of a group. Barry Prizant, PhD, notes that listening to people on the spectrum tells us that they desire social connection as much as anyone else.[1]

A Sense of Possibility: Art is about self-expression and possibility. To review, templates for the art projects are provided to set each child up for success (see Appendix C and SR-C.8). If someone has a different idea, please celebrate that. One boy used his decorated triangle to make a hat, another to fold and hang around his neck. As noted before, please normalize finishing a project at home. Many children create slowly for a variety of reasons. While you do need to closely keep to your yoga/art/yoga class schedule, no one should feel a limited sense of possibilities.

Benefits of Yoga

The science of the physical, emotional, and mental benefits of movement is discussed in Chapter 4: Yoga as a Healing Tool. Let's look at the benefits of the six poses included as art projects. Each pose can be practiced in a playful way, keeping the yoga both interactive and fun. Pose variations set everyone up for success. In addition, poses can be done seated, standing, or lying down. A child can also experience personal changes from one class to the next.

A Note: You can also provide many benefits by teaching the yoga program without the art component. You know your group. This flexible program can change to meet your planning needs.

Class 1: Triangle Pose builds body awareness, balance, and leg and core strength. Creating shapes with one's body builds a sense of where the body is in space (proprioception) and is fun.

Class 2: Rocket Pose is interactive and playful, so it builds social connection. A variation offers an opportunity to move the upper body from a grounded, stable base, which increases the strength and balance practice.

Class 3: Tree Pose improves balance, coordination, and confidence. It also strengthens the core and leg muscles. Simple variations (standing, sitting, or lying down) make it easy to adapt.

Class 4: Cobra Pose provides an opportunity to feel the pressure of the body against the floor. Gently (or firmly) pressing the hands down can change pressure sensations. Tapping the feet on the floor can build body awareness. Making soft sounds as you move adds more fun, creates more physical sensations, and teaches self-regulation.

Class 5: Peaceful Warrior Two Pose builds body awareness and a sense of where the body is in space. It also builds confidence, as it builds leg, core, and arm strength.

Class 6: Eagle Pose continues to build on the skills of the prior poses: balance, strength, and a sense of where the body is in space. It adds the important movement of crossing limbs (arms and legs) across the midline. A child can see improvement and growth over time but feel good about doing it the first time.

Benefits of Breathwork

To review this essential point: Breathwork is not an add-on. Rather, breathwork is a foundational component of any yoga practice. As noted, this program's five breathwork practices begin and end with simple movements: first pressing the shoulders back and then ending with a hand movement. But there is more. In between, the breathwork is paired with a simple movement (hands or feet, fingers or toes): "As YOU breathe in, stretch your fingers ..." The science of breathwork benefits is discussed in Chapter 4: Yoga as a Healing Tool. At least three reasons support pairing breathwork with a simple movement:

- Breathwork with a simple movement helps to build body awareness. This awareness can help a child to *feel* when they are getting upset or angry.

- Noticing how they *feel* sets a child up for the next step, to *practice* some simple breathwork to self-regulate.

- *Practicing* is an important part of *learning*. And again, to learn, someone must be paying attention.

This program's five breathwork practices include: 1) Feel the Breath; 2) The Open and Close Breath (Fist Breathing); 3) Balloon Breath; 4) The Counting Breath; and 5) It's a Wrap Breath (Chapter 14: Scripts for the Yoga Practice). It is important to note that each one is simple, quiet, and does not cause unpredictable shifts in affect (suddenly becoming agitated or suddenly feeling collapsed). It is also important to note that focusing on these five breathwork practices creates more opportunities for both children and adults to *practice* and then to *learn* from a base of the familiar. More is not better, more is confusing.

The Shanti the Monkey game (www.greentreeyoga.org/FREE) provides a fun game that guides and encourages children to use breathwork when they feel upset or to share a favorite breath with a friend or family member. The game was developed specifically for this population with special guidance from the founder of ABLE-differently (www.able-differently.org), Louis Allen, MD, FAAP, and Shelley Schwartz, MA, a teacher who worked with autistic children for over 30 years. (Many thanks!)

CHAPTER 12

Teaching Intentions

The GreenTREE Yoga® Approach

You have prepared the room. You have organized the children and adults. Now it is time to prepare for sharing yoga. First let's consider the teaching intentions as outlined in the 'Teaching Intentions' box below that build safety, support empowerment, and maintain simplicity. If this list looks long, that is because it is. But please notice that in the following tables and annotated scripts, using one phrase can cover many teaching intentions.

TEACHING INTENTIONS
Building Safety

1. Self-Regulation

2. Learning

3. Body Awareness

   3a. Grounding
   3b. Proprioception and Periphery
   3c. Twists

4. Predictable Yoga Sequences and Activities

5. Boundaries

6. The Value of Interactive Teaching

   6a. Social Engagement
   6b. Adapting for Your Group
   6c. Fun and Play

Supporting Empowerment

7. The Power of Choice

8. The Power of Phrasing and Pauses

    8a. Positive Phrasing
    8b. Pacing and the Pause

9. The Power of Physical Strength: Core/Balance

10. The Power of Normalizing

Maintaining Simplicity

11. Language

    11a. Simple, Consistent, and Literal
    11b. Repetition
    11c. The Sounds of Language

12. Simple Yoga

    12a. Simple Breathwork and Poses
    12b. Simple Instruction and Visual Cues

Suggested Phrases

The trauma-informed phrases in Tables 12.1, 12.2, and 12.3 meet the program goals of the GreenTREE Yoga® Approach as outlined in Part III: Building Safety, Supporting Empowerment, and Maintaining Simplicity. To underscore how a few simple words or phrases can strengthen your program, the numbers of the relevant teaching intentions from the 'Teaching Intentions' box are listed in the right-hand columns. These phrases accomplish these points without having to explain anything or creating verbal challenges and distractions. Reading through the tables, you may find phrases to make your program stronger and empower you to meet your changing program needs. Perhaps choose a few phrases that resonate with you, write them on your clipboard notes, and build your program from there. You have a wonderful opportunity to give children and their parents easy-to-use and valuable tools for physical, emotional, and mental health. You can decide if your extra effort is well-placed.

Table 12.1: Phrases to Build a Sense of Safety (Body Awareness/Self-Regulation)

Suggested Phrases	When to Use and Why It Builds a Sense of Safety	Supports These Teaching Intentions from the 'Teaching Intentions' Box
"We're glad you came to yoga …"	Begin and end each class with these words in the Hello Song and the Goodbye Song. Eases times of transitions.	(4) (6a) (6c) (11b)
"When you are ready, look at one hand. If you like, gently *wiggle* your fingers."	Builds body awareness and proprioception.	(3a) (3b) (7) (12a) (12b)
"… in any way that makes you *feel* strong today …"	Builds body awareness and a sense of mastery.	(3) (6c) (8a) (9)
"That's your yoga space."	Supports personal space/safety.	(3) (4) (5) (6c)
"When you are ready, gently press one shoulder back … Then press your other shoulder back."	Builds body awareness. Provides a consistent start to breathwork. Eases transitions.	(3a) (4) (11a) (11b)
"When you feel your leg muscles … when you feel your leg muscles, wiggle your fingers."	Encourages noticing strength.	(3a) (8b) (9) (10) (11b)
"When you are ready, look at one hand. If you like, gently *wiggle* the fingers on that hand or shake that hand."	Builds body awareness. Provides a consistent ending to breathwork.	(3a) (3b) (7) (11b) (12a) (12b)
"… a big, quiet lion yawn" "moo softly one time …"	Practices self-regulation.	(1) (2) (6a) (6b) (6c)
"Tap … tap … tap."	Builds body awareness.	(3) (3a) (3b) (6c) (11a) (11b) (12b)
"Who remembers what pose Shanti the Monkey practices next?"	Reinforces that the class is predictable and consistent.	(4) (6a) (6c)
"Let's practice 2 breaths."	Puts a boundary on the time.	(1) (2) (5)
"If you feel like being silly …" "Does that feel as silly as it looks?"	Having fun lowers stress levels.	(2) (6a) (6b) (6c) (7)

Table 12.2: Phrases to Support Empowerment

Suggested Phrases	When to Use and Why It Supports Empowerment	Supports These Teaching Intentions from the 'Teaching Intentions' Box
"When you are ready …" "If you like …"	Practice making a personal decision.	(1) (7) (8a) (10)
"Would you like to tap your leg 3 times … ?"	Practice making a personal decision.	(3a) (3b) (7)
"You know what to do …"	Offer on the second side of a pose or if a pose is repeated. Supports consistent/ predictable order and smoother transitions.	(2) (4) (6a) (6b) (7)
"There are many kinds of dogs, and there are many ways to practice the downdog pose." "Trees come in all shapes and sizes."	Normalizes differences.	(6a) (6b) (8a) (10)
"If *today* is a challenge day …"	Offers opportunity for personal growth.	(6c) (7) (9) (10)
"When you are ready, sit or stand tall …"	Gives choice as to how to do the pose. Normalizes differences.	(7) (10) (11a) (12b)
"… so you feel strong today." "Today you might feel stronger with your hand on the chair."	Encourages noticing strength.	(3) (9) (10) (12b)
"When you are ready, come to your hands and knees if you are not already there."	Normalizes differences.	(6a) (6b) (10) (12a) (12b)

Table 12.3: Phrases to Maintain Simplicity

Suggested Phrases	When to Use and Why It Maintains Simplicity	Supports These Teaching Intentions from the 'Teaching Intentions' Box
"We always do both sides."	No confusing right/left cues.	(11a) (12b)
"When you are ready, gently press one shoulder back ... Then press the other shoulder back."	Simple repetition allows for processing and then time to find the suggestion.	(3a) (4) (11a) (11b) (12a) (12b)
"Put one or both hands over your heart ... Put one or both hands over your heart."	Using the same phrase allows time to process and keeps your voice as a thread to safety.	(3a) (7) (8b) (11a) (11b)
"... *stretch* your fingers wide" "... *stretch* your arms wide"	Consistent cueing is easier to process and gives time to find the stretch.	(11a) (11b) (12b)
"If today is a challenge day ..."	Always using the same phrase supports ease of understanding.	(3a) (7) (8a) (10) (11a)
"Now Shanti the Monkey is *practicing* downdog." "Let's *practice* 2 breaths."	We are always practicing things. The word *practice* is used consistently to normalize differences and to avoid being directive.	(1) (2) (8a) (10)

CHAPTER 13

Class Format

Each class has five activities you can adapt for a 30/40-minute or a 60-minute class. The suggestion is to include all five activities in the art and yoga class. These 5 × 7-in/13 × 18-cm activity cards can be mounted on a foam core board (24 × 36-in/61 × 91-cm) to create your activity board (see Appendix B and SR-B.3).

	60 Minutes	Activities	40 Minutes
	5 minutes	**I. The Hello Song:** Class begins by engaging each child as you build social connection and body awareness. The Hello Song is sung quietly to greet each child. The child chooses a quiet finger snap or hand clap for all to do as they sing the personal greeting.	5 minutes
	15 minutes	**II. Yoga Part 1:** The Shanti the Monkey flip chart is on a stand next to you for visual cues and to assure there is a consistent and predictable class order as you move through the poses and breathwork (see SR-B.1).	10 minutes
	20 minutes (snack)	**III. Art:** The art project is based on the last pose of the class. The six-week program has six projects.	15 minutes
	10 minutes	**IV. Yoga Part 2:** The second yoga practice begins with the pose of the day, now with the art at the front of everyone's mat or carpet square. Practice the MP3 track here.	5 minutes
	10 minutes	**V. The Goodbye Song:** Class ends by engaging each child as you build social connection and body awareness. The Goodbye Song has the same format as the Hello Song.	5 minutes

I. The Hello Song

Introduce the Hello Song by pointing to the top card (Shanti the Monkey's smiling face) on the activity board. A special thanks to Shelley Schwartz who insisted I include songs. Trusting her 30 years of working with autistic children, I put my resistance aside. Thinking of it as more of a cheerful chant rather than as a tune to carry can allay the anxiety among those of us who can't sing. I will note that it worked out well and I had ... fun.

Connecting with Song: Going around your circle or room includes everyone. A child can choose a hand movement everyone can do as you sing. "Let's practice a soft clap ... a soft finger snap ... a soft pat (on legs). Okay, Kaya chose finger snaps." Everyone can snap their fingers and sing: "Hello, Kaya. Hello, Kaya. Hello, Kaya. We're glad you came to yoga." And then, "Sam, would you like soft claps, snaps, or pats?" As appropriate, you can add *one* new choice to claps, snaps, and pats (a total of four choices, the first three always in the same order). The children often have ideas too. One new choice can be patting hands on legs or finger taps on shoulders. Tapping opposite hand(s) on opposite shoulder(s) or leg(s) is another. Each reflects an awareness of sensory issues and builds on a base of the familiar. But remember: More is not better, more is confusing.

Building More Social Connection: If someone joins class later, it builds social connection and a sense of safety to pause and welcome that child by name in the Hello Song. Please know that it can be challenging for a parent or caregiver to get a child ready to leave and then to arrive on time. That warm welcome means you have not added to someone's stress.

Predictable and Consistent: Including the same question in the Hello Song provides structure and consistency. After the first class, the Hello Song ends with, "Who shared yoga with someone this week, maybe at home or at school?" Sometimes it can be appropriate to say, "Let's go around our circle (or the room)." If no one shares, your cheerful response can be, "Well, maybe today we will do something you'd like to share this week."

Activity Board: Again, point to the Hello Song card: "We did our Hello Song." Point to the Shanti the Monkey in tree pose on the activity board: "Now let's practice some yoga."

II. Yoga Part 1

It's important to maintain the same order of the Shanti flip chart from class to class. The following poses are represented on the flip chart that is next to you as you teach (Appendix A; SR-B.1). The teaching script for these poses is in Chapter 14: Scripts for the Yoga Practice. Please note that the same Shanti the Monkey card is used for all breathwork (top left Shanti in Table 13.1).

Table 13.1: Shanti the Monkey Cards in Flip Chart (Purple Monkeys)

Order for Flip Chart Cards

- Lion Pose

- Breathwork

- Seated Twist

- Butterfly

- Cat/Cow

- Snowball/Snowflake

- Downdog

- Mountain/Star

- Pose of the Day
  Class 1: Triangle Pose
  Class 2: Rocket Pose
  Class 3: Tree Pose
  Class 4: Cobra Pose
  Class 5: Peaceful Warrior Two
  Class 6: Eagle Pose

Activity Board: Point to each card: "We did the Hello Song. We practiced yoga. And now, it's time for our art project. Let's go to the art table and start with a snack."

III. Art

Reviewing the section on organizing the art project in Chapter 5: Preparations can set you up for success.

Activity Board: Point to each card again: "We did the Hello Song. We practiced yoga. We had a snack and did our art project. Now let's do more yoga."

IV. Yoga Part 2

The second yoga practice was not part of my initial sequence. But to my delight, the children wanted more yoga time. Turns out it provides a valuable review, a chance to display the artwork, and is ... fun. Again, adjust the time based on the number of poses you have added to the first yoga practice to match the art projects). It may be that yoga part 2 only has time for the first two suggestions:

1. Practice the pose of the day with the art project at the front of each mat or carpet square.

2. Practice one MP3 yoga break (see SR-D) to create familiarity with the break so a child can practice by themselves or with a parent.

3. Ask if someone would like to suggest a favorite pose for everyone to practice again. "Let's do three suggestions." Create that time boundary.

4. Ask if someone would like to teach their favorite pose. Create a time boundary.

Activity Board: Point to each card: "We did the Hello Song. We practiced yoga. We did our art project. We did more yoga. Now let's sing the Goodbye Song."

V. The Goodbye Song

Predictable and Consistent: Beginning with the same invitational question provides structure and consistency, easing the potential stress of transition times: "What yoga would you like to share with someone this week?" Or "Let's go around our circle (or the room). When it's your turn, you may like to share. But today may not be a day for that."

Connecting through Song: Now it's time to sing the Goodbye Song. Again, the Goodbye Song can be as simple as: "Marcos, what would you like us to do as we sing—quiet claps, snaps, or pats?" Everyone quietly claps as you all sing: "Goodbye, Marcos. Goodbye, Marcos. Goodbye, Marcos. We're glad you came to yoga." If a child leaves early, build social connection by pausing and singing them the Goodbye Song. It is important for everyone to *feel* seen and to *feel* acknowledged as part of your group.

Activity Board: Again, point to each card: "We sang the Hello Song. We practiced yoga. We had a snack and did our art project, we did more yoga, and we sang the Goodbye Song. Let's do more yoga next week! Look for the email (or whatever you are using) on Tuesday with the new Shanti the Monkey coloring sheet and yoga break." (See 'Stay Connected' in the 'Teaching Intentions' section in Chapter 6: Building Safety.)

A Final Note

When I first started this program, I stuck the activity cards on a foam core board with Velcro. Having only worked with neurotypical children, I had what I thought was a fun idea. If you envision this scenario, you may see at what point my plan went terribly awry. After we finished each activity, I asked if someone would like to take that card off the board. That's it, that's the scenario to envision. There are at least five reasons why that one suggestion is wrong.

1. Children are on the move, perhaps walking over someone's mat to get to board.

2. The stable, predictable visual cue (the activity board) is being taken apart, piece by piece. How could I say as I pointed to the activity board, "We've done the Hello Song, we've done yoga ..."?

3. The cards may be askew, as they aren't firmly on the board. Someone may fixate on the fact one card is farther apart from the others or on a slight angle.

4. Someone may feel left out because they had wanted to be chosen.

5. Velcro makes noise. The lesson I learned was to keep front and center in my teacher's mind that these are not *neuro*typical groups.

A Note: We cannot control everything in the room, a fact that makes controlling what we can even more important.

CHAPTER 14

Scripts for the Yoga Practice

Setting up for Success

To support your teaching, full scripts for these breathwork practices and yoga poses are provided. Downloads are available in SR-C.2. Clipboard notes (see Appendix D and SR-C.3) for that class placed next to you provide an easy reference for timing the class and phrases you want to include. And again, a clipboard sends the message that you are organized and care about your teaching. Let's quickly review some key teaching points. Why all the quick reviews? Because these key points strengthen your program.

Physical Variations: Many of the poses can easily be done seated or standing. The suggestion is to say the seated cue first (even if no one is seated), both to be inclusive and to let everyone in the room know that sitting is an option at any time during the practice. "When you are ready, come back to sitting or standing tall." In addition, many poses can also be done lying down. The option of standing against a wall may be appropriate for individual sessions, depending on the physical and grounding needs of the child. But in groups, moving to a wall can add commotion and disruption to an already organized space. In groups, having a chair already placed at the back of each yoga space (mat or carpet square) offers support without disrupting the room arrangement. You may have noted that this program is highly adaptable.

Predicable and Consistent: As discussed, teaching the poses and breathwork in the same order on the flip chart provides reassurances of a predictable and consistent class. Both visual and auditory cues support smoother transitions. The predictable and consistent language in the written scripts provides a strong starting point for your program. As you read through the scripts, it can be interesting to notice how reading the words makes you *feel*. That's a sentence to read again, as it gets to the heart of this program. How do the suggestions, the words, the phrases, and the ideas make you *feel*? A talented yoga teacher shared that she first familiarizes herself with the language by reading the scripts aloud as she does the yoga poses and breathwork. (Thank you, Rebecca!) And again, have fun.

Adjustments and Variations: As a child learns the poses, the pace may change. As mentioned before, you can adjust your pace as you assess the individual or group responses. For more able groups, you can add variations to build on a base of the familiar. What remains constant is the teaching language and the teaching intentions: safety, empowerment, and simplicity.

Literal and Fun: Can your cues be both literal and fun? And does it matter? Yes, and yes. Let's start with why it matters. As mentioned before, reaching your branches toward the sky can be a distracting cue. Your teaching guide, quite literally, is to say what you mean. "Do you feel like being silly today?" has the fun factor covered. "Wiggle your fingers ... wiggle your toes ... and even wiggle your nose," is literal and fun. "Are you still wiggling?" As noted, some children will keep wiggling the next week, knowing that question is coming. More silliness can be, "Pretend you are a ...." You have said what follows is pretending. It's a positive teaching practice for any group, as many children benefit from the practice of differentiating between what is real and what is pretend.

Breathwork Practices

The suggestion is to choose two breathwork practices for each class. Feel the Breath is the simplest one. It may also be used as a two-breath pause between poses. No flip chart card is needed.

Boundaries Matter: The breathwork can be for 2 or 3 breaths as meets the group needs (age/ability/attention levels). Stating the number of times you are going to practice the breath helps the children know what to expect.

Name It: Naming the breath keeps your teaching consistent and predictable. "Let's practice Balloon Breath 3 times."

Clutter-Free: The suggestion is to use the same wording for each breath. Extra words are more ideas to process. Clear, consistent cues support the teaching intention of children experiencing different types of breathwork without distractions. In this way, they may find one to practice later or to share with others.

Begin and End with Same Cues: To review, breathwork begins with the same cue: "When you are ready, gently press one shoulder back ... Then press the other shoulder back." Breathwork always ends with gently moving the hands in some way. Beginning and ending with the same cues or phrases does at least five things; it:

- creates predictability and consistency and can help ease the stress of transitions

- sets up a better physical posture for breathing (shoulders back)

- provides more grounding opportunities through body awareness

- provides physical, visual, and auditory signals that breathwork is ahead

- empowers through practicing making choices.

It's Not a Race: The suggestion is to be mindful that children usually have more shallow breathing than adults. How do you match their breathing? Don't try. "As YOU breathe in ..." supports children building breath and body awareness as they find their own breathing patterns. It is also another way to set everyone up for success.

The Bonus Round: After more able children are familiar with the breathwork, adding *one* breath fact can keep it interesting. Two facts to share (*one* per breathwork) are: 1) longer breaths in *can* be energizing; or 2) longer breaths out *can* be calming. Please note the use of the word *can*. It's not helpful to tell someone how they will or should feel. The intention, again, is to provide the opportunity to *feel* the breath.

Quick and Quiet: It's worth repeating because it works. A quick way to get the room quiet is to put your hands over your heart (visual cue only) and simply say, "Okay, everyone. Listen for your breath. That's right, listen for your breath." In 2 breaths the room is usually quiet.

Annotated Scripts

To appreciate more fully what these phrases can bring to your teaching, let's first look at an annotated sample page of the class introduction, one breathwork practice, and one yoga pose from these scripts. The numbers after each sentence indicate the teaching intentions from the 'Teaching Intentions' box. I have not listed every intention so that you might add some too. Why give yourself the time to do this exercise? Because it clearly shows that one simple sentence can relay many positive points, all without the clutter of extra words or ideas. It clearly shows that: More is not better, more is confusing. It also makes your teaching much easier. You can read the script, refer back to the phrase charts if you like, and then decide if this approach strengthens and supports your teaching intentions.

Introduction (6a) (6b) (11c)

1. "I am glad you came to yoga today. (*Point to activity board.*) (6a) (11c) Let's start by sitting on a carpet square (mat or a chair). (3a) (4) (5) Wiggle around to get comfortable in your seat if you like ... wiggling to one side and then wiggling to the other side. (3a) (3b) (6c) (7) Now, would you like to sit very still ... with no wiggles? (1) (7)

2. When you are ready, look at both hands. (3a) (3b) (7) (11a) (12b) If you like, stretch your fingers wide. (3b) (7) Now tap your fingertips 3 times in front of you. Tap ... tap ... tap. (1) (3b) (8b) (11b) (12b) Would you like to stretch your arms to one side? And you know what to do ... If you like, tap 3 more times. (1) (3b) (3c) (8a) (11b) (12b) Tap ... tap ... tap. And when you are ready, stretch your arms to the other side and tap 3 more times ... Tap ... tap ... tap. Can you tap your back? You pick how many taps for today. (1) (3b) (3c) (11b) (12b)

3. When you are ready, come back to facing front. (3b) (7) (11a) (11b) That's your yoga space." (3a) (5) (8a) (11a) (12b)

Lion Pose (6a) (6b) (11c)

1. "We always begin yoga practicing lion pose like Shanti the Monkey. (4) (6c) (*Point to the flip chart.*) When YOU *feel* your big breath in ... stretch your arms out to the side or over your head. (3b) (6b) (8a) When YOU *feel* your big breath out ... stretch forward. (11a) (12a) (12b) Do you want to stretch your arms to one side ... then stretch your arms to the other side? (3b) (3c) (7)

2. When you are ready, come back to sitting tall. (3b) (4) (7) (11a) (12b)

3. If you like, look at one hand. Would you like to stretch these fingers today? (3b) (7) Then look at your other hand. Would you like to stretch those fingers today? (3b) (7) If today is a challenge day, stretch the fingers on both hands at the same time. (3b) (6b) (8a) After your fingers *feel* all stretched out, put your hands on your legs. (3a) (3b) (7)

4. Would you like to be silly today? (6a) (6c) (7) Can you stick out your tongue? Now, that's silly. (6a) (6c) (11b) Okay, when you *feel* your big

breath in ... open your mouth in a big, quiet lion yawn. When you *feel* your big breath out ... you can stick out your tongue like Shanti the Monkey. (1) (6c) (7) (11a) (11b) (12b) Does that *feel* as silly as it looks? (6a) (6c) Should we practice lion pose one more time? You know what to do. (2) (7) When you *feel* your big breath in ... open your mouth in a big, quiet lion yawn. When you *feel* your big breath out ... you can stick out your tongue like Shanti the Monkey. (1) (6c) (7) (11a) (11b) (12b) Now, that's silly! When you are ready, come back to sitting tall." (3a) (7)

Variations: After several weeks, you can vary the size of 3 quiet lion yawns by cueing a small yawn, then a big lion yawn, then any size yawn they choose. (1) (6c) (7)

Feel the Breath (6a) (6b) (11c)

1. "When you are ready, gently press one shoulder back ...

   Then press the other shoulder back. (4) (7) (8b) (11b)

2. Put one or both hands over your heart ...

   Put one or both hands over your heart (8b) (11a) (11b)

3. Let's practice Feel the Breath 2 (or 3) times. (1) (4) (5)

   Feel the breath in ... Feel the breath out. (1) (4) (8b) (11a) (11b)

   (*Repeat slowly for each breath.*)

4. When you are ready, look at one hand. (3a) (3b) (7) (8b) (11a) If you like, gently *wiggle* the fingers on that hand or shake that hand. (3a) (3b) (6c) (7) Then look at your other hand. Would you like to wiggle the fingers on that hand or shake that hand? (3a) (3b) (6c) (7). How still would you like to hold your hands today? (1) (3a) (7)

5. You might want to practice Feel the Breath later when you want to feel better or to get to sleep." (1) (2) (7)

Yoga Scripts

Introduction

1. "I am glad you came to yoga today. Let's start by sitting on a carpet square (mat or a chair). Wiggle around to get comfortable in your seat if you like … wiggling to one side and then wiggling to the other side. Now, would you like to sit very still with no wiggles?

2. When you are ready, look at both hands. If you like, wiggle one finger on each hand. Now tap your fingertips 3 times in front of you. Tap … tap … tap. Would you like to stretch to one side? If you like, tap 3 more times. Tap … tap … tap. And when you are ready, stretch to the other side. And you know what to do … If you like, tap 3 more times. Tap … tap … tap. Can you tap behind you? When you are ready, come back to facing front. That's your yoga space.

3. When you are ready, gently press one shoulder back … Then press the other shoulder back. Each time we do yoga we will do the same poses from the Shanti the Monkey flip chart. (*Point to flip chart.*) Then, each week we can add our new pose of the day. That new pose will be our art project." (*Point to activity board.*)

Lion Pose

1. "We always begin yoga practicing lion pose like Shanti the Monkey. (*Point to the flip chart.*) When YOU *feel* your big breath in ... stretch your arms out to the side or over your head. When YOU *feel* your big breath out ... stretch forward. Do you want to stretch your arms in a different way?

2. When you are ready, come back to sitting tall.

3. If you like, look at one hand. Would you like to stretch these fingers today? Then look at your other hand. Would you like to stretch those fingers today? If today is a challenge day, stretch one hand and then the other, going back and forth. After your fingers feel all stretched out, put your hands on your legs.

4. Would you like to be silly today? Can you stick out your tongue? Now, that's silly. Okay, when YOU *feel* your big breath in ... open your mouth in a big, quiet lion yawn. When YOU *feel* your big breath out ... stick out your tongue like Shanti the Monkey. Does that feel as silly as it looks? Should we practice lion pose one more time? You know what to do. When you *feel* your big breath in ... open your mouth in a big, quiet lion yawn. When you *feel* your big breath out ... stick out your tongue like Shanti the Monkey. Now, that's silly! When you are ready, come back to sitting tall. (**Variation**)

5. Who remembers what Shanti the Monkey practices next?"

(*Flip to next card.*)

Variation: After several weeks, you can vary the size of 3 quiet lion yawns by cueing a small yawn, then a big lion yawn, then any size yawn they choose. It is better to vary the size and not the sounds of the yawn. Loud lion roars are not a good choice, as many children are very sensitive to low tones. Many thanks to Dawn Young, E-RYT for this engaging variation.

Breathwork

Choose *one* of these breathwork practices to start each class, but each is the *same* Shanti card.

Feel the Breath

Feel the Breath is the simplest breathwork. The suggestion is to teach it at least twice in each class.

1. "When you are ready, gently press one shoulder back …

   Then press the other shoulder back.

   Put one or both hands over your heart …

   Put one or both hands over your heart.

2. Let's practice Feel the Breath 2 (or 3) times.

   Feel the breath in … Feel the breath out. (*Repeat slowly for each breath.*)

   When you are ready, look at one hand. If you like, gently *wiggle* the fingers on that hand or shake that hand … Then look at your other hand. Gently *wiggle* the fingers on that hand or shake that hand. How still would you like to hold your hands today? (**Variation**)

3. You might want to practice Feel the Breath later when you want to feel better or to get to sleep.

4. Who remembers what pose Shanti the Monkey practices next?"

   (*Flip to next card on chart.*)

Variation: For more able groups, first gently *wiggle* the fingers on one hand, then gently *stretch* the fingers on the other hand.

Open and Close Breath (Fist Breathing)

1. "If you like, move around in your seat so you feel comfortable today.

2. When you are ready, gently press one shoulder back …

   Then press the other shoulder back.

3. Let's practice the Open and Close Breath 2 (or 3) times.

As YOU breathe in, fingers close ... As YOU breathe out, fingers open. (*Use the same wording for each breath.*) (**Variation**)

4. When you are ready, look at one hand. If you like, gently *move* the fingers on that hand or shake that hand ... Then look at your other hand. Gently *move* the fingers on that hand or shake that hand. How still would you like to hold your hands today?

5. Who remembers what pose Shanti the Monkey practices next?"

(*Flip to next card on chart.*)

Variations:

1. Teaching it as Fist Breathing may be appropriate. "As YOU breathe in, make gentle fists ... As YOU breathe out, release." Children may like to name the breath: Rock/flower breath is one name.

2. After children are familiar with the breath, introduce closing the fingers (or fists) firmly or gently.

Balloon Breath

(Generously shared by Dawn Young, E-RYT.)

1. "When you are ready, gently press one shoulder back ...

   Then press the other shoulder back.

2. If you like, put your fingertips together as though you are holding a small balloon.

   As YOU breathe in, pretend the balloon is filling with air. As YOU breathe out, press your hands together, pressing the air out of the balloon.

3. Let's practice Balloon Breath 2 (or 3) times.

   As YOU breathe in, hands apart ... As YOU breathe out, hands press together. (*Use the same wording for each breath.*) (**Variation**)

4. Today you may want to wrap the fingers on one hand around the fingers on the other hand ... Wrap the fingers on one hand around the fingers on other hand. If you like, press down on your fingers. (**Variation**)

5. Would you like to try that on the other hand? Okay, wrap your fingers

around your other hand ... Wrap your fingers around your other hand. If you would like to, press down on your fingers.

6. When you are ready, look at both hands. If you like, gently *move* the fingers on both hands or shake both hands. Now, how still would you like to hold your hands today?

7. You can practice Balloon Breath when you start to feel upset, or maybe you can teach it to someone at home.

8. Who remembers what pose Shanti the Monkey practices next?"

(*Flip to next card on chart.*)

Variation: After children are familiar with the breath, introduce the choice of a firm or a gentle press on the fingers or fingertips.

Counting Breath

1. "When you are ready, gently press one shoulder back ...

   Then press the other shoulder back.

2. If you like, put one or both hands over your heart ...

   Put one or both hands over your heart.

3. Let's practice the Counting Breath 3 times.

   As YOU breathe in, fingers press ...

   As YOU breathe out, release the press. That's one.

   As YOU breathe in, fingers press ...

   As YOU breathe out, release the press. That's two.

   As YOU breathe in, fingers press ...

   As YOU breathe out, release the press. That's three.

4. When you are ready, look at one hand. If you like, gently *move* the fingers on that hand or shake that hand ... Then look at your other hand. If you like, gently *move* the fingers on that hand or shake that hand. Now, how still would you like to hold your hands today?

5. Who remembers what pose Shanti the Monkey practices next?"

   (*Flip to next card on chart.*)

It's a Wrap Breath

1. "If you feel like being silly, wiggle your arms all around ... wiggle your arms all around.

2. **Side 1:** When you are ready, wrap your arms around yourself.

   Side 2: When you are ready, put your other arm on top as you wrap your arms around yourself.

3. Let's practice 2 It's a Wrap Breaths.

   As YOU breathe in, press down on your hands ...

   As YOU breathe out, release the press. (*Say 2 times slowly.*)

4. **Side 1:** If you feel like being silly again, stretch your arms wide and wiggle your fingers. We always do both sides.

   Side 2: If you still feel like being silly, stretch your arms wide and do something that *feels* silly today.

5. When you are ready, look at one hand. If you like, gently *move* the fingers on that hand or shake that hand ... Then look at your other hand. Gently *move* the fingers on that hand or shake that hand. Now, how still would you like to hold your hands today? (**Variation**)

6. Who remembers what pose Shanti the Monkey practices next?"

   (*Flip to next card on chart.*)

Variation: "Gently *move* the fingers on one hand ... gently *wiggle* the fingers on the other hand."

Seated Twist

1. "When you are ready, stretch your arms to the side or over your head ... Stretch your arms to the side or over your head. If you like, wiggle your fingers all around. Today you might want to wiggle the rest of you too. Wiggle your fingers, wiggle your shoulders, maybe even wiggle your nose. Does that feel silly? When you are ready, bring your arms down. Are you *still* wiggling?

   (*You may find that some children remember that question the next week, so they keep wiggling in amusement.*)

2. We always do both sides. Let's practice a twist like Shanti the Monkey. When you are ready, bring both hands across to one side ... Bring both hands across to one side. Today you might want to press down on your *hands*. When you are ready, come back to facing front.

3. If you like, wiggle your fingers all around. If you feel like being silly again, wiggle the rest of you all around again. Wiggle your fingers, wiggle your shoulders, maybe even wiggle your *toes*. When you are done with your wiggling, how still can you sit today?

4. Now let's practice a twist to the other side. You know what to do. When you are ready, bring both hands across to the other side ... Bring both hands across to the other side. Today on this side, you might want to press down on your *fingertips*. When you are ready, come back to facing front.

5. Today you may want to gently *wiggle* the fingers on one hand or shake that hand ... Then gently *wiggle* the fingers on the other hand or shake that hand. If you like, look at your hands. How still would you like to hold your hands today?

6. Who remembers what pose Shanti the Monkey practices next?"

   (*Flip to next card on chart.*)

Butterfly

This pose can be done seated in a chair or on the floor. Only the cues for moving the legs change. If done lying down, begin with the feet on the floor under bended knees.

1. "There are many different sizes and shapes of butterflies. We can sit in butterfly pose, either on a chair or on the floor. If you like, you can move your knees (*side to side for those sitting in a chair or lying down, and up and down for those sitting on the floor*) as you *pretend* to flap like a butterfly. Then let your legs be as still as you would like them to be.

2. Now if you like, press your fingers on your shoulders. Today you might want to flap your arms, pretending they are butterfly wings. Can you feel your muscles as you gently flap? If you were a butterfly, where would you like to fly?

3. If you want to be even sillier today, flap your knees and flap your arms at the same time. Moving your arms and your legs can make you stronger. And when you are ready, stop flapping one arm ... Then stop flapping the other arm ... Then let your hands rest in your lap. Are you *still* flapping your legs? (*You may find that some children remember that question the next week, and they are still flapping in amusement.*) When you are ready, be very still like a butterfly resting on a flower. Who has a butterfly fact they would like to share? (*See enthusiasms on p. 58*)

4. When you are ready, wiggle around in your seat until it feels comfortable to you. If you like, put one or both hands over your heart ... Put one or both hands over your heart. Listen for your breath ... that's right, listen for your breath. (*Give time for 2–3 breaths.*)

5. When you are ready, look at one hand. If you like, gently *flap* the fingers on that hand ... Then look at your other hand. Gently *flap* the fingers on that hand. Would you like to flap both hands? That's silly. Now, how still would you like to hold your hands today?

6. Who remembers what pose Shanti the Monkey practices next?"

   (*Flip to next card on chart.*)

Cat/Cow Pose

This pose can be done seated by pressing the hands down on the legs.

Cat Pose

1. "Shanti the Monkey is practicing cat pose. If you have seen a cat do this stretch, wiggle one thumb.

2. When you are ready, if you are sitting, put your hands on your legs … or come down to your hands and knees. Can you tap one foot (or one hand) 3 times? Tap … tap … tap. Then tap the other foot (or hand) 3 times? Tap … tap … tap. How still would you like to hold your feet (or hands)? (**Variation 1, 2, or 3**)

3. Can you meow softly one time like a cat? Now let's stretch like a cat. *Feel* your big breath in … and as you *feel* your breath out … tuck your chin and arch your back … tuck your chin and arch your back. If you like, meow *softly* one time. When you are ready, sit tall in your chair or come back to your hands and knees with a flat back.

4. Who remembers what pose we practice next?"

   (*Flip to next card on chart.*)

Variations:

1. "If you like, tap your hand (or foot) gently (or firmly) today."

2. "If you like, tap your hand on one side and your foot on the other side." (*Remember to do the other side.*)

3. "You choose how many times you would like to tap your fingers today."

Cow Pose

1. "Shanti the Monkey is practicing cow pose. Can you use your finger to show the new shape of Shanti's back?

2. Can you moo softly one time? Now let's stretch like a very old and tired cow. As YOU breathe in, lift your chin and lift your tail-bone … As YOU breathe out, moo one time *softly*. When you are ready, sit tall in your chair or come back to your hands and knees with a flat back.

3. Should we do cat and cow one more time? (*Repeat cat/cow.*)

4. When you are ready, find a comfortable seat. Today you may want to wiggle around in your seat … Then sit as still as you would like to sit. Are you still wiggling? If you like, gently press one shoulder back … Then press the other shoulder back.

5. When you are ready, put your hands over your heart …

   Put your hands over your heart.

6. Let's practice Feel the Breath 2 times.

   Feel the breath in …. Feel the breath out. (*Say 2 times slowly.*)

7. When you are ready, look at one hand. If you like, gently *stretch* the fingers on that hand or shake that hand … Then look at your other hand. Gently *stretch* the fingers on that hand or shake that hand. Now, how still would you like to hold your hands today?

8. Who remembers what pose Shanti the Monkey practices next?"

   (*Flip to next card on chart.*)

Snowball/Snowflake Pose

Both poses can also easily be done seated, with the arms wrapping around the shoulders in snowball pose. Then, the arms can open wide into snowflake pose.

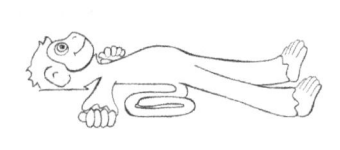

1. "Shanti the Monkey is practicing snowball pose. Would you like to be silly and pretend you are a snowball? If you are sitting, wrap your arms around your shoulders. If you are lying down, find a comfortable way to wrap yourself into a pretend snowball.

2. Let's practice Feel the Breath 2 times in snowball pose.

   Feel the breath in ...

   Feel the breath out. (*Say 2 times slowly.*) (**Variation 1 or 2**)

3. Now if you like, stretch your arms and legs as wide as you like. We can call this snowflake pose. Stretch your fingers wide ... If you want, stretch your toes wide. That's silly.

4. Should we be silly one more time? If you like, make your snowball one more time. You might want to press your hands more firmly. When you are ready, stretch out into snowflake pose again. Can you press your heels down on the floor? If you like, stretch your fingers and stretch your toes into a really big snowflake.

5. When you are ready, find a comfortable seat. Give yourself time to move from side to side to find your comfortable seat. Then sit as still as you would like to sit today.

6. When you are ready, gently press one shoulder back ... Then press the other shoulder back. If you like, put one or both hands over your heart ... Put one or both hands over your heart.

7. Let's practice Feel the Breath 2 (or 3) times.

   Feel the breath in ... Feel the breath out. (*Say 2 or 3 times slowly.*)

8. When you are ready, look at both hands. Gently *stretch* all your fingers or shake your hands. Now, how still would you like to hold your hands? (**Variation 3**)

9. Who remembers what pose Shanti the Monkey practices next?"

   (*Flip to next card on chart.*)

Variations:

1. To make the snowball bigger, some groups might like to rock from front to back, from side to side, or even around in a circle (you might want to try it at home first to experience the feeling and then demonstrate the options.)

2. After several classes, add *one* option of gently pressing down on the hands or wiggling the feet (or toes).

3. Ask for ideas on new names for the snowball/snowflake sequence or ask for two snowflake facts. (*See enthusiasms p. 58.*)

Downdog

Downdog can be done with the hands on the back of the chair as someone steps back and then releases forward a comfortable distance. Downdog can also be done on hands and knees.

1. "Now Shanti the Monkey is practicing down-dog. Wiggle your thumb if you have seen a dog do this stretch, maybe after a nap. There are many kinds of dogs, and there are many ways to practice the downdog pose. You might stand behind a chair[1] (*demonstrate*). Today you might come down onto your hands and knees. Or you can lift your hips like Shanti the Monkey.

2. Wherever you are, can you wiggle from side to side? You may want to bark *softly* one time as you wiggle from side to side. If today is a challenge day, lift one leg up and move it around in any way that feels comfort-able ... Lift one leg and move it around in any way that feels comfortable. When you are ready, put that leg down. Now lift the other leg and move it around. Move that leg in a way that feels comfortable today. When you are ready, put that leg down.

3. Can you find a new downdog stretch today? Should we all bark *softly* one more time?

4. When you are ready, find a comfortable seat. Look at one hand. If you like, gently *wiggle* the fingers on that hand or shake that hand ... Then look at your other hand. Gently *wiggle* the fingers on that hand or shake that hand. Now, how still would you like to hold your hands today?

5. Who remembers what pose Shanti the Monkey practices next?"

(*Flip to next card on chart.*)

Tall Mountain/Star Pose

Tall Mountain Pose

1. "Shanti the Monkey is practicing tall mountain pose. Let's sit or stand tall. You can stretch your arms out to the side or over your head. Today you might want to stretch your fingers wide.

2. If today is a challenge day, can you lift one heel? As you move around and find your balance, you are getting stronger. Can you lift the other heel? If you lift both heels, you might feel yourself smile. When you are ready, put your hands on your hips. If you like, press down on your fingers." (**Variation**)

Variation: Vary the press (gentle or firm). **Or:** Strum or tap the fingers on the hips.

Star Pose

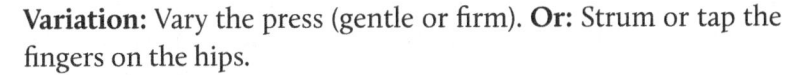

1. "Now let's pretend to be a shining star. If you like, move or jump your feet apart ... Then stretch your arms wide ... Today you might want to wiggle your fingers.

2. The star pose challenge is to move your arms in any way that *feels* like you are using a lot of energy, like a shining star.

3. When you are ready, move or jump your feet together. Sit or stand in tall mountain pose again. (*Choose one of these questions—see enthusiasms p. 58.*) Who has a favorite star or constellation? Who would like to share an interesting fact about stars?

4. When you are ready, look at one hand. If you like, gently *stretch* the fingers on that hand or shake that hand ... Then look at your other hand. Gently *stretch* the fingers on that hand or shake that hand. Would you like to stretch the fingers on both hands? Now, how still would you like to hold your hands?

5. Who remembers what pose Shanti the Monkey practices next?"

   (*Flip to next card on chart.*)

Pose of the Day

Class 1: Triangle Pose

This pose can be done standing, seated on a chair, or lying down (feet on the floor under the knees, arms can lift to touch the knees for triangle shapes).

1. "What shapes can you see Shanti the Monkey making? Let's make triangles as we move in triangle pose. We always do both sides. You can sit tall on one side of your chair ... or you can stand tall on your mat.

2. If you like, make a gentle fist with one hand. Would you like to tap your leg 3 times? Tap ... tap ... tap. Now move or step that leg back. Can you stretch that same arm over your head? If you like, press your other hand on the chair or your leg to make another triangle. Wherever your arm is today, stretch your fingers wide.

3. When you are ready, come back to sitting or standing tall with your hands on your hips.

4. Now let's wrap the fingers on one hand around the fingers on the other hand. Then if you like, press on your fingers. Would you like to try that on the other hand? When you are ready, wrap your fingers around your other hand. Then if you like, press on your fingers. (**Variation 1**) If you like, gently shake both hands.

5. Okay, let's make more triangle shapes. When you are ready, make a gentle fist in your other hand. And you know what to do. Tap your other leg 3 times. Tap ... tap ... tap. Now move or step that leg back. Can you stretch that arm over your head? Can you make even more triangle shapes? When you are ready, sit or stand tall.

6. If you like, look at one foot. Then gently *shake* that foot ... Then look at your other foot. Gently *shake* that foot. Then, how still would you like to be today? (**Variation 2**)

7. Who remembers what pose Shanti the Monkey practices next?

   (*Flip to next card on chart.*) **Or:** (*If this is the last pose of yoga part 1*) Who knows what we do after yoga?" (*Point to activity board.*)

Variations:

1. Cue a gentle or firm press.

2. "If you would like another challenge today, use your fingers on both hands and make more triangles. Can you make the triangles different sizes? (*Model stretching your fingers on one hand. Use a finger on the other hand across those fingertips to make triangles.*) Can you make other shapes as you move your fingers?"

Class 2: Rocket Pose

Rocket pose can be done with the back knee on the floor or seated on the side of a chair.

1. "Shanti the Monkey is doing rocket pose. There are many kinds of rockets. Find a rocket pose that makes you *feel* strong today. We always do both sides. When you are ready, sit tall on one side of your chair or stand tall. Can you stretch one hand and wiggle your fingers? Now tap your leg (*outside leg for those seated on the side of chair*) 3 times with those fingers. Tap ... tap ... tap. Then move or step that leg back. If you like, bend your front knee. You might want to rest your hand above your knee today.

2. Wiggle your fingers on your top hand. If you want to be silly in rocket pose, put that palm by your ear. We can *quietly* count, 3-2-1 blast off as your arm takes off over your head. Let's blast off 3 times. (**Variation**)

3. When you are ready, come back to sitting or standing tall with your hands on your hips. Gently press one shoulder back ... Then press the other shoulder back.

4. Let's practice Finger Press Breaths 2 times.

   As YOU breathe in, fingers press ...

   As YOU breathe out, release the press. (*Say 2 times slowly.*)

   Variation: Someone may know another language. That person counts on the first round, then you all count together the second and third time.

   (*Repeat rocket pose on the other side.*)

5. *Choose one way to finish this pose based on the ability levels of your group*:

   a. When you are ready, gently *move* the fingers on one hand or shake that hand … Then gently *move* the fingers on the other hand or shake that hand. Now, how still would you like to hold your hands?

   b. If you like, press your palms together … One hand can blast off as fast as you would like. Let's blast off 2 more times.

   (*Repeat with the other hand.*)

6. Who has a rocket fact to share? (*See enthusiasms on p. 58.*) Who remembers what pose Shanti the Monkey practices next?

   (*Flip to next card on flip chart.*) **Or:** (*If this is the last pose of yoga part 1*) Who knows what we do after yoga?" (*Point to activity board.*)

Class 3: Tree Pose

Tree pose can be done seated on a chair, standing, or lying down.

1. "Shanti the Monkey is doing tree pose. Trees come in all shapes and sizes. When you are ready, sit or stand tall. Set yourself up so you *feel* strong today.

2. We always do both sides. If you like, *wave* one hand. Can you tap your leg 3 times with that hand? Tap … tap … tap. When you are ready, turn that knee open like Shanti the Monkey. You can keep your toes on the ground today. If today is a challenge day, you can press your foot against the standing leg. Today you may feel stronger with your hand on the chair.

3. Do you feel like being silly?

   Side 1: You can pretend your arms are tree branches moving in the wind. Is it a strong wind today? Now, that's silly. We always do both sides.

   Side 2: Can you move around in tree pose until you smile? We are still being silly.

4. **Side 1:** When you are ready, come back to sitting or standing tall. Today you might want to shake one leg 3 times. Shake … shake … shake. Then shake your other leg 3 times. Shake … shake … shake. Now, how still would you like your legs to be? Let's practice tree pose on the other side. (*Repeat above.*)

Side 2: When you are ready, come back to sitting or standing tall. (*Choose one of these questions—see enthusiasms on p. 58.*) Who knows a tree that is very strong? What trees bend in the wind? What trees have roots growing in the water? Who would like to share an interesting fact about a tree?

5. If you like, gently press one shoulder back ... Then gently press the other shoulder back. Let's practice the Finger Stretch Breath 2 times. As YOU breathe in, fingers *stretch* ... As YOU breathe out, release the stretch. (*Say 2 times slowly.*)

6. When you are ready, look at one hand. If you like, gently *wave* the fingers on that hand or shake that hand ... Then look at your other hand. Gently *wave* the fingers on that hand or shake that hand. Now, how still would you like to hold your hands today?

7. Who remembers what pose Shanti the Monkey practices next?

   (*Flip to next card on flip chart.*) **Or:** (*If this is the last pose of yoga part 1*) Who knows what we do after yoga?" (*Point to activity board.*)

Class 4: Cobra

Many thanks to Dawn Young, E-RYT, for delighting us with her cobra sequence. Cobra pose can also be done seated (floor or chair) with hands pressing on the legs.

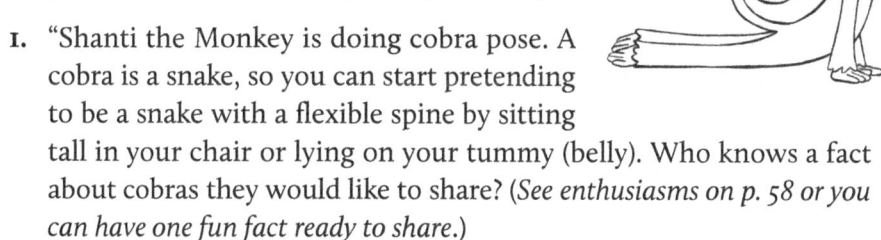

1. "Shanti the Monkey is doing cobra pose. A cobra is a snake, so you can start pretending to be a snake with a flexible spine by sitting tall in your chair or lying on your tummy (belly). Who knows a fact about cobras they would like to share? (*See enthusiasms on p. 58 or you can have one fun fact ready to share.*)

2. If you are sitting, put one hand on your tummy (belly). If you are lying down, feel your tummy (belly) on the floor. Now *feel* your tummy (belly) as YOU breathe in ... *Feel* your tummy (belly) as YOU breathe out. If you like, tap one foot 3 times. Tap ... tap ... tap ... Then tap the other foot 3 times. Tap ... tap ... tap. If today is a challenge day for you, wiggle all your toes. Can you tap and wiggle your toes at the same time? That's silly.

3. When you are ready, if you are sitting, put your hands on your legs. If you are lying on your tummy (belly), put your hands on the floor under your shoulders. Let's practice 3 cobra breaths.

a. When YOU *feel* a *little* breath in ... press up into baby cobra like Shanti the Monkey ... When YOU *feel* your breath out, release down.

b. When YOU *feel* a *bigger* breath in ... press up into big kid cobra ... When YOU *feel* your breath out, release down.

c. When YOU *feel* a *very big* breath in ... press up into the biggest cobra you can be. When YOU feel your breath out, release down.

4. If you like, tap *both* feet 3 times. Tap ... tap ... tap. Do you want to wiggle all your toes again? When you are done wiggling, how still would you like your feet to be? Should we do cobra pose one more time?

(Repeat above.)

5. When you are ready, sit tall. If you like, gently press one shoulder back ... Then gently press the other shoulder back. Today you may want to put your hands over your heart. Let's practice Feel the Breath 2 times.

Feel the breath in ... Feel the breath out. (*Say 2 times slowly.*)

6. Now, when you are ready, look at one hand. If you like, gently *move* the fingers on that hand or shake that hand ... Then look at your other hand. Gently *move* the fingers on that hand or shake that hand. How still would you like to hold your hands today? (**Variation**)

7. Who remembers what pose Shanti the Monkey practices next?

(*Flip to next card on flip chart.*) **Or:** (*If this is the last pose of yoga part 1*) Who knows what we do after yoga?" (*Point to activity board.*)

Variation: Move one hand like a slithering snake ... move the other hand like that slithering snake.

Class 5: Peaceful Warrior Two

Peaceful warrior two can be done seated on a chair or standing.

1. "Shanti the Monkey is doing peaceful warrior two. When you are ready, sit tall on one side of your chair or stand tall. We always do both sides. If you like, *stretch* the fingers on one hand ... then *wiggle* the fingers on that same hand. Then tap those fingers on your leg 3 times. Tap ... tap ... tap. When you are ready, move or step that leg back like Shanti the Monkey.

2. Today you might want to stretch both arms. Or today you may want to put your hands on your hips. Find a peaceful warrior that makes you feel strong today.

3. If you like, bend your front knee. When you feel your muscles working ... when you feel your muscles working, wiggle your *nose*. When you are ready, put your hands on your hips. If you like, press down on your fingers. (**Variation**)

4. When you are ready, sit or stand tall. If you like, gently *move* the fingers on one hand or *shake* that hand ... Then gently *move* the fingers on the other hand or shake that hand.

5. Now let's be strong, peaceful warriors on the other side.

    (*Repeat 1–4. Then go to 6.*)

6. When you are ready, put one or both hands over your heart ... Put one or both hands over your heart. Let's practice Feel the Breath 2 times.

    Feel the breath in ... Feel the breath out. (*Say 2 times slowly.*)

7. Who remembers what pose Shanti the Monkey practices next?

    (*Flip to next card on flip chart.*) **Or:** (*If this is the last pose of yoga part 1*) Who knows what we do after yoga?" (*Point to activity board.*)

Variation: Vary the press (gentle or firm). **Or:** Strum or tap the fingers on the hips.

Class 6: Eagle Pose
Eagle pose can be done standing, seated on a chair, or lying down.

1. "Shanti the Monkey is doing eagle pose. Let's sit or stand tall. If you like, press down on your toes. Now you might want to wiggle your toes. Did you know that baby eagles need to learn to fly? Are you *still* wiggling your toes? That's silly.

2. Let's start eagle pose by pretending we are baby eagles learning to fly.

    When YOU *feel* your big breath in ... lift your arms like wings. Then when YOU *feel* your big breath out, bring your arms down. Should we do that one more time? (*Repeat slowly.*)

3. Now let's pretend to be bigger eagles. We always do both sides. If you like, stretch your fingers on one hand. Can you tap your leg 3 times with that hand? Tap ... tap ... tap. It's a silly pose, because eagles don't cross their legs. When you are ready, cross that leg around your other leg. Finding your balance makes you stronger.

4. If you like, put one or both hands over your heart. Today you may feel stronger with your hand on the chair. (**Variation 1 or 2**)

5. When you are ready, come back to sitting or standing tall. If you like, gently flap the fingers on one hand, then gently flap the fingers on the other hand.

6. When you are ready, put one or both hands over your heart ...

   Put one or both hands over your heart.

7. Let's practice Feel the Breath 2 times.

   Feel the breath in ... Feel the breath out. (*Say 2 times slowly.*)

8. Now let's be strong eagles standing on the other leg.

   (*Repeat 2–7 on the other side, then go to 9.*)

9. *Choose one way to end this pose based on the ability levels of your group.*

   a. When you are ready, gently *move* the fingers on one hand or shake that hand ... Then gently *move* the fingers on the other hand or shake that hand. If you like, look at your hands. How still would you like to hold your hands today?

   b. If you like, wrap the fingers on one hand around the fingers on the other hand in a new way.

   Can you find a new way to wrap using all your fingers?

10. Who knows what we do after yoga?" (*Point to activity board.*)

Variations:

1. "Practice stacking the elbows while standing on two feet or sitting tall."

2. "If today is a challenge day, practice bringing one leg around and stacking the elbows, like Shanti the Monkey."

CHAPTER 15

Six Art Projects

Please review the suggestions on organizing and teaching the art projects in Chapters 5 and 6. These ideas can support you in building a stronger program.

Class 1: Triangle Pose

Materials

- File folders, triangle template (see Appendix C and SR-C.8)
- Materials for triangles
- School glue/glitter glue, popsicle sticks
- Hole punch, scissors, colored markers
- Yarns of various colors and textures
- Several small white paper plates (or plastic lids) to hold the glue
- Large white paper plate for each child for craft materials and to mark their spot
- Envelopes to take materials home as needed

Your Preparation

1. Trace and cut triangle templates from file folders. Always cut extra.

2. Punch three holes in the top of each triangle so you can thread the yarn through the top.

3. Cut 18-in (45-cm) lengths of various yarns. Some may want to include yarn in their designs, so bring extra.

4. Cut triangles of various sizes, colors, textures. Keep them separated by size/texture/material.

5. Create your own triangle design as an example to show the possibilities. Put yarn through the top of the triangle to show how they can be hung and displayed.

6. Before class, put glue on several small white paper plates so it's ready to use.

7. Arrange the sorted triangle materials in the center of the table and set out the large paper plates.

The Activity

1. Children choose their triangle materials (varied yarns, triangles) to put on their paper plate.

2. Give each child a triangle template on which to glue triangle shapes.

3. Hold up an envelope and let children know they can take materials to finish at home.

4. Set the triangles aside or on the front of the yoga mats to dry. Yoga part 2 includes the pose of the day with the art project near the child.

Class 2: Rocket Pose

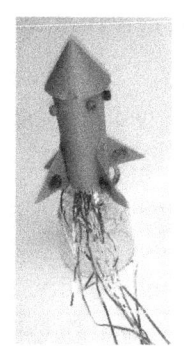 

Materials

- Thick construction paper/card stock of various colors (or toilet paper rolls for the body)

- Template for nose cone, wings, body (see Appendix C and SR-C.8)

- Beads, sequins, red and silver tinsel

- Markers, school glue, popsicle sticks, scissors

- Several small white paper plates (or plastic lids) to hold the glue

- Large white paper plate for each child's craft materials and to mark their spot

- Envelopes to take materials home as needed

Your Preparation

1. Trace and cut nose cones, wings, and the rocket body from various colors of construction paper or card stock.

2. Create your sample rocket.

3. Before class, put glue on several small white paper plates so it's ready to use.

4. Arrange the sorted rocket materials in the center of the table and set out the large paper plates.

The Activity

1. Children choose their rocket materials from the center of the table to put on their plates.

2. Fold and glue the nose cone and wings to the body of the rocket.

3. Decorate the body of the rocket.

4. Glue tinsel to the inside of the base.

5. Set the rockets aside or on the front of the yoga mats to dry. Yoga part 2 includes the pose of the day with the art project near the child.

Class 3: Tree Pose

Materials

- File folders, tree template (see Appendix C and SR-C.8)

- Tissue paper (various colors)

- School glue, popsicle sticks, scissors, crayons/colored markers

- Several small white paper plates (or plastic lids) to hold the glue

- Large white paper plate for each child's craft materials and to mark their spot

- Envelopes to take materials home as needed

Your Preparation

1. Cut 3-in (8-cm) tissue paper squares for the leaves (separated by colors).

2. Trim each folder so it has four even sides when open (no folder tabs on indents, see p. 159). Draw tree outlines in the center. (Draw extra.)

3. Create your sample tree project.

4. Before class, put glue on each small white paper plate so it's ready to use.

5. Arrange the sorted tree materials in the center of the table and set out the large paper plates.

The Activity

1. Children choose tree art materials to put on their plates. Give each child a tree template.

2. To make the leaves from a 3-in (8-cm) square of tissue paper: Take a square of tissue paper and either roll it into a ball or make a small circle with one hand by curling the forefinger into the thumb and then use your finger to push a piece of tissue paper through the hole to make a leaf.

3. Glue the leaves on the tree.

4. With markers, add decoration to the tree background, including wildlife or activities.

5. Put the trees on the front of the yoga mats to dry. Yoga part 2 includes the pose of the day with the art project near the child.

Class 4: Cobra Pose

Note: This project needs several adults helping.

Materials

- Large white athletic socks

- Large white paper plate for each child's craft materials and to mark their spot
- Hot glue/glue gun
- Markers for fabric, glitter glue
- Wiggly eyes (craft store)
- Very thick elastic bands
- Rice or beans
- Red, yellow, or orange pipe cleaners, preferably the kind with feathered edges

Your Preparation

1. Make a sample cobra.

2. Cut the pipe cleaners to 6-in (15-cm) lengths.

3. Arrange the sorted cobra materials in the center of the table and set out the large paper plates.

The Activity

1. Children choose their cobra art materials to put on their plates.

2. Give each child a sock to decorate.

3. Adults help with:

    a. gluing on the eyes (glue gun)

    b. poking the pipe cleaner from the inside for the tongue

    c. filling the sock ¾ full with rice or beans

    d. securing the end with a thick elastic band (a thin elastic band will break).

4. Put the cobras on the front of the yoga mats to dry.

Class 5: Peaceful Warrior Two Pose

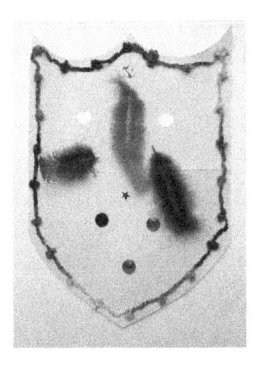 

Materials

- File folders, template (see Appendix C and SR-C.8)
- School glue/glitter glue
- Markers, stapler, popsicle sticks
- Yarn, feathers, sequins, stickers
- Several small white paper plates (plastic lids) to hold the glue
- Large white paper plate for each child's craft materials and to mark their spot
- Envelopes to take materials home as needed

Your Preparation

1. Trace and cut out the templates from the file folders; shields and handles (4 × 10-in (10 × 25-cm) strips). (Make extra.)
2. Make your warrior shield.
3. Before class, put glue on each small white paper plate so it's ready to use.
4. Arrange the sorted shield materials in the center of the table.

The Activity

1. Children choose the peaceful warrior materials to put on their plates. Give each child a shield template.
2. Decorate the shields in a way "that makes them feel strong."

3. Staple the handle to the back of the shield.

4. Put the shields on the front of the yoga mats to dry. Yoga part 2 includes the pose of the day with the art project near the child.

Class 6: Eagle Pose

Materials

- File folders/cardboard, eagle template (see Appendix C and SR-C.8)
- Brown and white feathers, yellow foam for bill
- School glue, scissors
- Wiggly eyes, brown textured felt
- Extra cardboard, markers to support for eagle variations (feet/legs)
- Several small white paper plates (plastic lids) to hold the glue
- Large white paper plate for each child's craft materials and to mark their spot
- Envelopes to take materials home as needed

Your Preparation

1. Cut out the brown felt pieces, eagle bills, and eagle body templates.

2. Create your eagle art.

3. Before class, put glue on each small white paper plate so it's ready to use.

4. Arrange the sorted eagle materials in the center of the table and set out the large paper plates.

The Activity

1. Children choose the eagle art materials to put on their plates. Give each child the eagle template.

2. Glue the brown felt to the template.

3. Glue the feathers, eyes, and bill to the template.

4. Put the eagles on the front of the yoga mats to dry. Yoga part 2 includes the pose of the day with the art project near the child.

PART VI

APPENDICES

Shanti Flip Chart (sample)

To download color versions of the cards to print, see SR-B.1.
Print at 8.5 × 11 in (A4 paper).

Activity Board (sample)

To download color versions of the card to print, see SR-B.3.
Print at 5 × 7 in (13 × 18 cm).

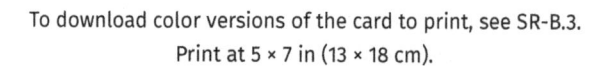

Mount on poster board
24 × 36 in (61 × 91 cm) and
place on a small stand.

Art Templates

To download the templates to print, see SR-B.3.

Class 1: Triangle

Print at 8.5 × 11 in (A4 paper).

Print the template, trace it on to a file folder, cut out the triangle, and open to use. The dotted line of the triangle template should be placed on the fold of the file folder.

Class 2: Rocket

Print at 8.5 × 11 in (A4 paper).

Print the template, trace it on to cardboard, and cut out the colored paper pieces.

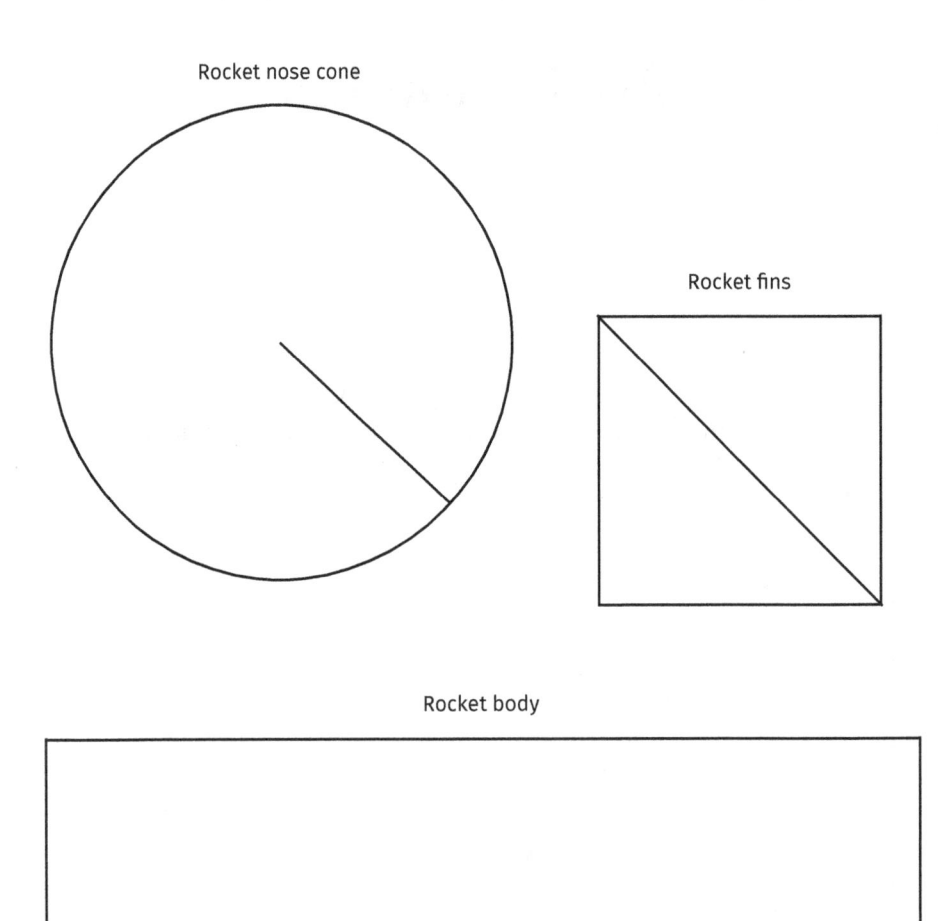

Rocket nose cone

Rocket fins

Rocket body

Class 3: Tree

Print at 11 × 17 in (A3 paper).

Print the template, trace it on to a file folder, and cut out the tree.

Class 5: Peaceful Warrior Two

Print at 11 × 17 in (A3 paper).

Print the template, trace it on to a file folder or card, and cut out the warrior shield.

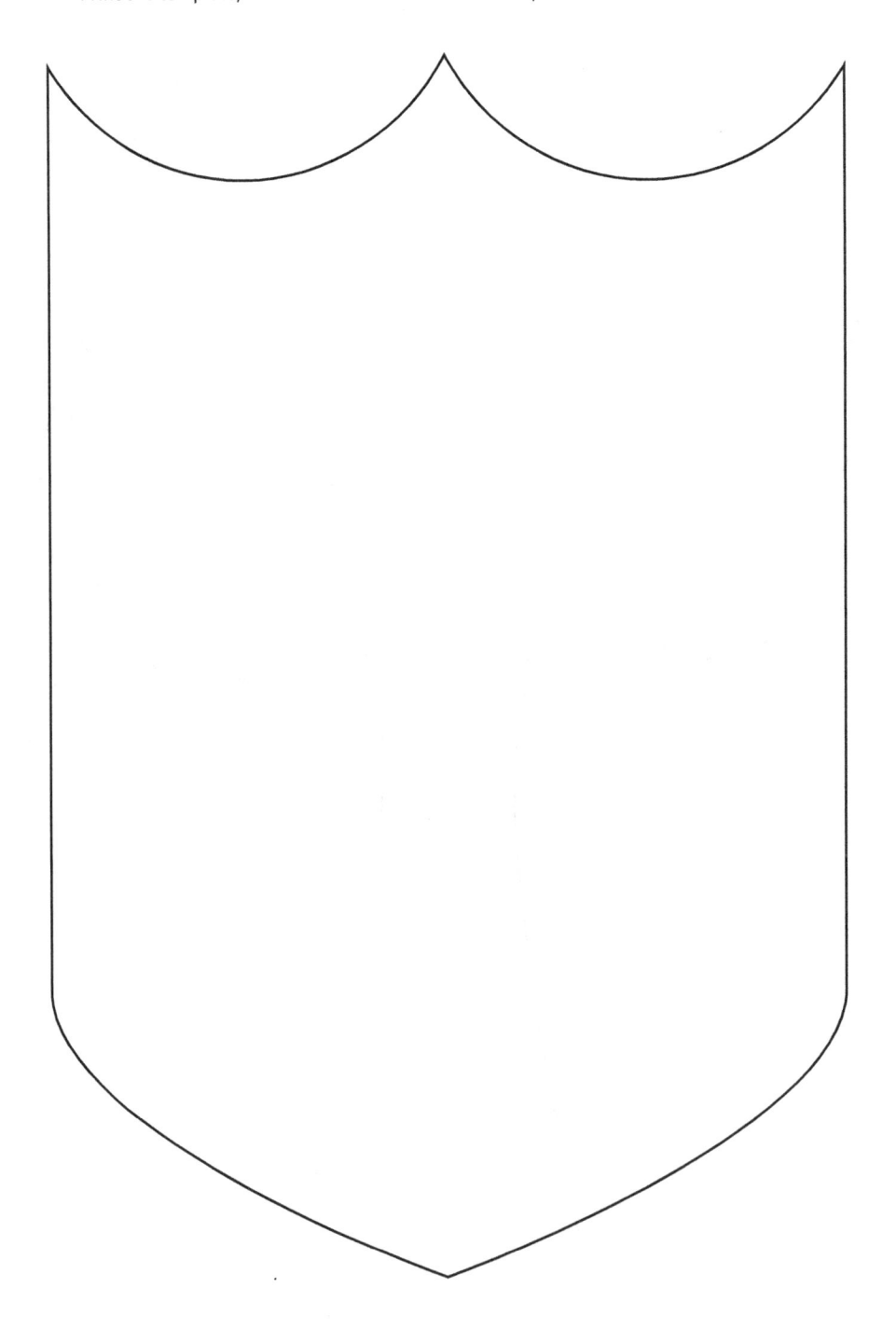

Class 6: Eagle

Print at 8.5 × 11 in (A4 paper).

Print the template, trace it on to a file folder or card, and cut out each piece.

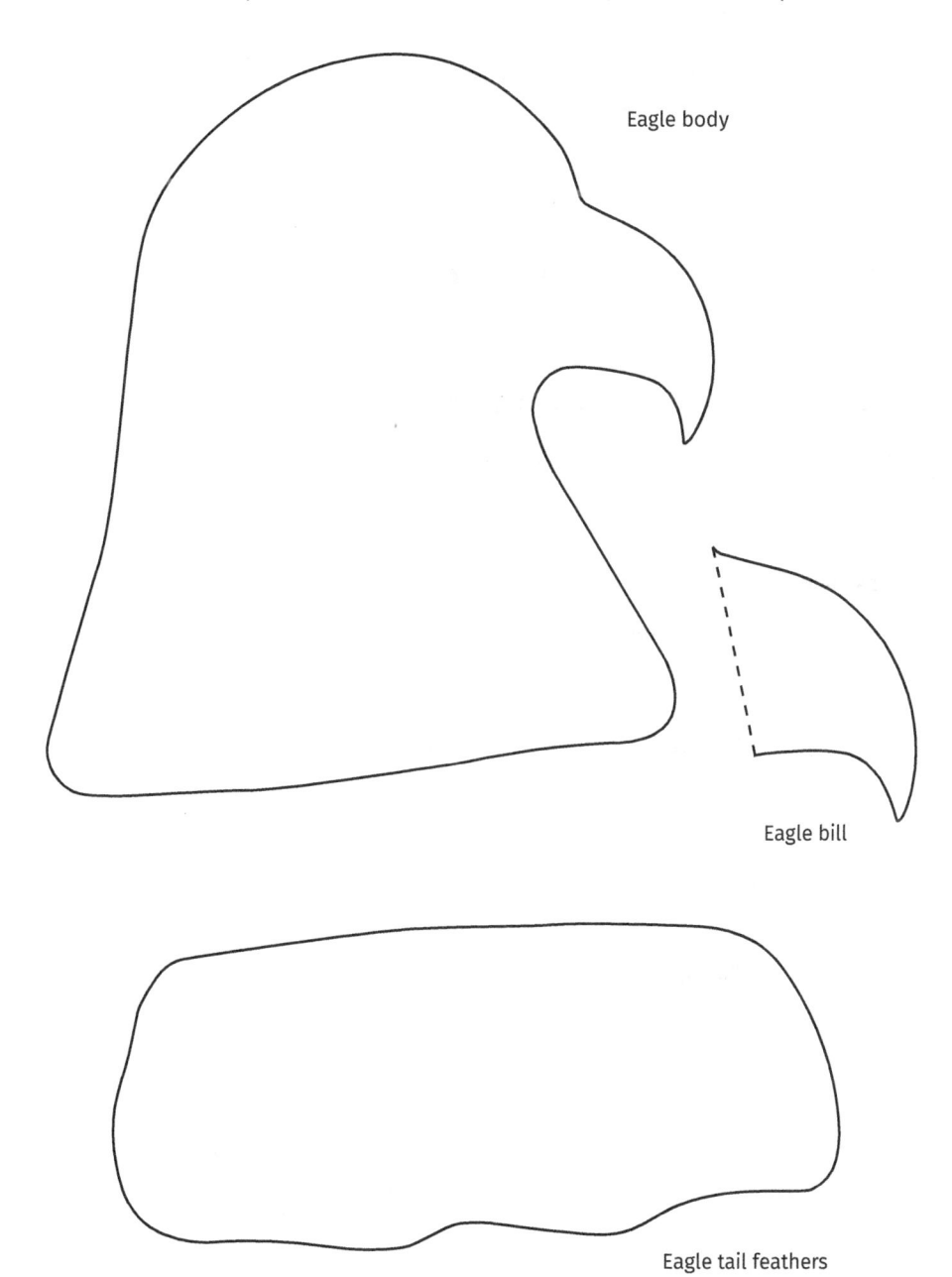

Eagle body

Eagle bill

Eagle tail feathers

Clipboard Notes

Appendix D.1 One Class

CLIPBOARD NOTES

Class # _____   **Art Project** _____

Class Time:		**Your Notes:**
I. _____	**I. Hello Song** (_____ min)	**I. Hello Song** a. Hello Song b. Pose/breath shared at home
II. _____	**II. Yoga** (_____ min)	
III. _____	**III. Art** (_____ min)	**Phrases to Use:**
IV. _____	**IV. Yoga** (_____ min)	**IV. MP3 break:**
V. _____	**V. Goodbye Song** (_____ min)	**V. Goodbye Song** a. What pose/breath to share at home b. Goodbye Song

Appendix D.2 MP3 Schedule

Suggestions of MP3s to play during yoga part 2

	Art Project	Breathwork	MP3 Break for Yoga Part 2
Class 1	Triangle	Gentle Fist Breathing	5. Breathing Seated Twist and Gentle Fist Breathing (3 minutes)
Class 2	Rocket	Balloon Breath	9. Tapping and Balloon Breath (2 minutes)
Class 3	Tree	Strong Fist Breathing	1.A. Tree Pose with Strong Fist Breathing (5 minutes)
Class 4	Cobra	Balloon Breath	2.A. Cobra with Balloon Breath (5 minutes)
Class 5	Peaceful Warrior 2	Counting Breath	4.A. Peaceful Warrior 2 with Counting Breath (5 minutes)
Class 6	Eagle	Strong Fist	7. Seated Tall Mountain with Strong Fist Breathing (3 minutes)

Sample Flyer

ART & YOGA
Summer Fun for Children
with Differing Needs or Autism

What allows kids to have fun, focus,
manage stress, and build strength
and balance all at the same time?
It's yoga!

Have summer fun with your child as
you learn simple yoga and create art
projects together.

Includes breaks to practice at home.

Who: Children who can follow simple directions.
Parents, please plan to attend.

Where: The Children's Center

When: Wednesdays 6/20–8/1: 10:30–11:30 a.m. or 12:30–1:30 p.m.
Childcare available for $xx.00 per sibling.

Register by June 1 at (email) or (phone).

Contact xx with any questions.

Shanti Coloring Sheets

Resources: Books, Websites, Podcasts

Books on Autism and Differing Needs

Goldberg, Louise (2013) *Yoga Therapy for Children with Autism and Special Needs*. New York: W. W. Norton & Company.

Grandin, Temple (2023) *Different Kinds of Minds: A Guide to Your Brain*. New York: Philomel.

Grandin, Temple (2023) *Visual Thinking: The Hidden Gifts of People Who Think in Pictures, Patterns, and Abstractions*. New York: Riverhead Books.

Grandin, Temple, and Moore, Debra (2021) *Navigating Autism: 9 Mindsets for Helping Kids on the Spectrum*. New York: W. W. Norton.

Grandin, Temple, and Panek, Richard (2014) *The Autistic Brain: Helping Different Kinds of Minds Succeed*. Boston: Mariner Books.

Miller, Lucy Jane (2014) *Sensational Kids: Hope and Help for Children with Sensory Processing Disorder (SPD)*. New York: TarcherPerigree.

Prizant, Barry, M. (2022) *Uniquely Human: Updated and Expanded: A Different Way of Seeing Autism*. New York: Simon and Schuster. (See SCERTS® Model below.)

Silberman, Steve (2016) *Neurotribes: The Legacy of Autism and the Future of Neurodiversity*. New York: Avery.

Books on Neuroscience/Neuroplasticity

Doidge, Norman (2016) *The Brain's Way of Healing: Remarkable Discoveries and Recoveries from the Frontiers of Neuroplasticity*. New York: Penguin Life.

Porges, Stephen (2017) *The Pocket Guide to the Polyvagal Theory: The Transformative Power of Feeling Safe*. New York: W. W. Norton. (Discusses autism.)

Porges, Stephen (2021) *Polyvagal Safety: Attachment, Communication, Self-Regulation. Norton Series on Interpersonal Neurobiology*. New York: W. W. Norton. (Discusses autism.)

Books on Exercise and Movement

Feldenkrais, Moshe (1972/77) *Awareness Through Movement*. New York: HarperCollins.

Ratey, John (2008) *Spark: The Revolutionary New Science of Exercise and the Brain*. New York: Little, Brown Spark.

Organizations/Websites with Programs and Support Resources

Autism Society: https://autismsociety.org

Autism Speaks: www.autismspeaks.org

Center for Parent Information and Resources: A hub serving parent centers that serve families of children with disabilities (US based): www.parentcenterhub.org

National Autism Association: https://nationalautismassociation.org

Parent to Parent USA: www.p2pusa.org/parents

Safe and Sound Listening Protocol: Stephen Porges, PhD, developed this evidence-based program to help foster and strengthen a sense of safety and to build social engagement system through sound. https://integratedlistening.com

SCERTS® Model: A research-based, comprehensive model focusing on social communication, emotional regulation, and transactional support. https://scerts.com Also see: https://scerts.com/wp-content/uploads/SCERTS_2pg_3_16.pdf

STAR Institute for Sensory Processing: A world leader in research, education, and therapy for differences in sensory processing. https://sensoryhealth.org/basic/why-choose-star

Temple Grandin, PhD: www.templegrandin.com

The Ed Asner Family Center: https://edasnerfamilycenter.org

Podcasts

Uniquely Human: www.uniquelyhuman.com

Episode 96 (1/5/24): Raising Neurodivergent Children of Color: A Discussion with Jaya Ramesh and Priya Saaral, Neurodivergent Parents and Professionals

Episode 98 (2/2/24): Temple Grandin on Understanding Different Minds: Its Importance in Education, Life Skills and Eventual Employment for Younger Autistic Individuals

Endnotes

Introduction

1   Prizant, B. (2015/2022) *Uniquely Human: A Different Way of Seeing Autism*. New York: Simon & Schuster. p. 116.

Chapter 1

1   Miller, L. J. (2006) *Sensational Kids: Hope and Help for Children with Sensory Processing Disorder (SPD)*. G. P. Putnams Sons. p. 5.
2   Ponzo, S. *et al.* (2019) Vestibular modulation of multisensory integration during actual and vicarious tactile stimulation. *Psychophysiology, 56*(10), e13431.
3   Ferrè, E. R. *et al.* (2020) Vestibular cognition: State-of-the-art and future directions. *Cognitive Neuropsychology, 37*(7–8), 413–420.
4   Miller, L. J. (2006) p. 31.
5   MacClean, P. (1990) *The Triune Brain in Evolution: Role in Paleocerebral Functions*. New York: Plenum.
6   Zimmer, C. (2023) The human brain has a dizzying array of mystery cells. *New York Times.* October 12.
7   Berlucchi, G. *et al.* (2009) Neuronal plasticity: Historical roots and evolution of meaning. *Experimental Brain Research, 192*(3), 307.
8   Kandel, E. (2007) *In Search of Memory: The Emergence of a New Science of Mind*. New York: W. W. Norton and Company. p. 395.
9   Doidge, N. (2007) *The Brain That Changes Itself: Stories of Personal Triumph from the Frontiers of Brain Science.* New York: Penguin Life.
10   Grandin, T. and Panek, R. (2013) *The Autistic Brain: Thinking Across the Spectrum.* Boston, MA: Houghton Mifflin Harcourt. p. 40.

Chapter 2

1   Ledoux, J. (2015) *Anxious: Using the Brain to Understand Fear and Anxiety*. New York: Viking Press. p. 210.
2   Porges, S. (2021) *Polyvagal Safety: Attachment, Communication, Self-Regulation (IPNB)*. New York: W. W. Norton. p. 12.
3   Porges, S. W. (1995) Orienting in a defensive world: Mammalian modifications of our evolutionary heritage: A Polyvagal Theory. *Psychophysiology, 32*, 301–318.
4   Porges, S. (2021) pp. 1–2.
5   Porges, S. (2021) pp. 138–139.
6   Prizant, B. (2015/2022) p. 19.

Chapter 3

1   Goldberg, L. (2013) *Yoga Therapy for Children with Autism and Special Needs.* W. W. Norton and Company. p. 10.

2 Ogundele, M. O. (2018) Behavioural and emotional disorders in childhood: A brief overview for paediatricians. *World Journal of Clinical Pediatrics*, *7*(1), 9-10.

3 Miller, L. J. (2006) p. 6.

4 Miller, L. J. (2006) p. 6.

5 Miller, L. J. (2006) p. 12.

6 Miller, L. J. (2006) p. 28.

7 Singer, J. (2017) *Neurodiversity: The Birth of an Idea*. Kindle ebook published by Judy Singer and printed in 2017. p. 17.

8 Leschziner, G. (2022) *The Man Who Tasted Words: A Neurologist Explores the Strange and Startling World of Our Senses*. New York: St. Martin's Press. p. 277.

9 Leschziner, G. (2022) p. 277.

10 Grandin, T. (2013) pp. 31-32.

11 Grandin, T. (2022) *Visual Thinking: The Hidden Gifts of People Who Think in Pictures, Patterns, and Abstractions*. New York: Riverhead Books. p. 223.

12 Silberman, S. (2015) *Neurotribes: The Legacy of Autism and the Future of Neurodiversity*. New York: Avery. p. 12.

13 Maenner, M. J., Warren, Z., Williams, A. R. et al. Prevalence and Characteristics of Autism Spectrum Disorder Among Children Aged 8 Years — Autism and Developmental Disabilities Monitoring Network, 11 Sites, United States, 2020. *MMWR Surveill Summ 2023*, *72*(2), 1-14.

14 Brockevelt, B. *et al.* (2013) A comparison of the Sensory Profile scores of children with autism and an age- and gender-matched sample. *South Dakota Medicine: Journal of the South Dakota State Medical Association*, *66*(11), 459, 461, 463-465.

15 Habayeb, S. *et al.* (2023) A multisystem approach to improving autism care. *Pediatrics*, *152*(5), e2022060584.

16 O'Nions, E. *et al.* (2023) Autism in England: Assessing underdiagnosis in a population-based cohort study of prospectively collected primary care data. *Lancet Regional Health: Europe*, *29*, 100626.

17 Posar, A. *et al.* (2015) Autism according to diagnostic and statistical manual of mental disorders 5(th) edition: The need for further improvements. *Journal of Pediatric Neurosciences*, 10(2), 146-148.

18 Hess, P. (2022) DSM-5 revision tweaks autism entry for clarity. *Spectrum Autism Research News*. March 17.

19 Evans, B. (2013) How autism became autism: The radical transformation of a central concept of child development in Britain. *History of the Human Sciences*, *26*(3), 3-31.

20 Wing, L. (1996) *The Autistic Spectrum*. London: Constable and Robinson. p. 20.

21 Waltz, M. (2015) Mothers and autism: The evolution of a discourse of blame. *AMA Journal of Ethics*, *17*(4), 353-358.

22 Silberman, S. (2015) p. 105.

23 Vitello, P. (2014) Dr. Lorna Wing, who broadened views of autism, dies at 85. *New York Times*. June 19.

24 Silberman, S. (2015) p. 353.

25 Singer, J. (2017) p. 31.

26 Silberman, S. (2015) p. 468.

27 Silberman, S. (2015) p. 7.

28 Xie, S. *et al.* (2019) Family history of mental and neurological disorders and risk of autism. *JAMA Network Open*, *2*(3), e190154.

29 Taylor, M. J. *et al.* (2020) Etiology of autism spectrum disorders and autistic traits over time. *JAMA Psychiatry*, *77*(9), 936-943.

30 Satterstrom, F. K. *et al.* (2020) Large-scale exome sequencing study implicates both developmental and functional changes in the neurobiology of autism. *Cell*, *180*, 568-584.

31 Grandin, T. (1995/2006/2010) *Thinking in Pictures: My Life with Autism*. New York: Vintage Books. p. 5.

32 Silberman, S. (2015) p. 470.

33 Porges, S. (2017) *The Pocket Guide to the Polyvagal Theory: The Transformative Power of Feeling Safe*. New York: W. W. Norton. pp. 77–78.

34 Porges, S. (2021) *Polyvagal Safety: Attachment, Communication, Self-Regulation*. New York: W. W. Norton. pp. 77–78, 206.

35 Grandin, T. (1995/2006) pp. 28–29.

36 Grandin, T. (2022) p. 35.

37 Silberman, S. (2015) p. 470.

38 Ben-Sasson, A. *et al.* (2009) A meta-analysis of sensory modulation symptoms in individuals with autism spectrum disorders. *Journal of Autism and Developmental Disorders*, *39*(1), 1–12.

39 Ahn, R. R. *et al.* (2004) Prevalence of parents' perceptions of sensory processing disorders among kindergarten children. *American Journal of Occupational Therapy*, *58*(3), 287–293.

40 Tomchek, S. D. *et al.* (2007) Sensory processing in children with and without autism: A comparative study using the short sensory profile. *American Journal of Occupational Therapy*, *61*(2), 190–200.

41 Porges, S. (2021) p. 206.

42 See https://integratedlistening.com for more on Dr. Porges listening project.

43 Silberman, S. (2015) p. 472.

44 Leschziner, G. (2022) p. 264.

45 Dance, C. J. *et al.* (2022) The prevalence of aphantasia in the general population. *Consciousness and Cognition*, *97*, 103243.

46 Miller, L. J. (2006) pp. 31, 37.

47 Miller, L. J. (2006).

48 Prizant, B. (2015/2022) p. 4.

Chapter 4

1 Feldenkrais, M. (1981/2019) *The Elusive Obvious: The Convergence of Movement, Neuroplasticity and Health*. Berkeley, CA: North Atlantic Books. p. 92.

2 Desikachar, T. K. V. (1999). *The Heart of Yoga*. Rochester, VT: Inner Traditions. p. 17.

3 Feldenkrais, M. (1972/1977/1990) *Awareness Through Movement*. New York: HarperOne. pp. 36–37.

4 Lieberman, D. E. (2021) *Exercised: Why Something We Never Evolved to Do Is Healthy and Rewarding*. New York: Pantheon Books. p. 64.

5 Emery, C. F. *et al.* (2005) Exercise accelerates wound healing among healthy older adults. *Journals of Gerontology. Series A, Biological Sciences and Medical Sciences*, *60*(11), 1432–1436.

6 Berrueta, L. *et al.* (2016). Stretching impacts inflammation resolution in connective tissue. *Journal of Cellular Physiology*, *231*(7), 1621–1627.

7 Lieberman, D. E. (2021) p. 268.

8 Basso, J. C. *et al.* (2017) The effects of acute exercise on mood, cognition, neurophysiology, and neurochemical pathways: A review. *Brain Plasticity*, *2*(2), 127–152.

9 Young, S. N. (2007) How to increase serotonin in the human brain without drugs. *Journal of Psychiatry & Neuroscience*, *32*(6), 394–349.

10 Ratey, J. (2008/2013) *Spark: The Revolutionary New Science of Exercise and the Brain*. New York: Little, Brown Spark. p. 102.

11 Lieberman, D. E. (2021) p. 64.

12 Ratey, J. (2008/2013) p. 7.

13 Merzenich, M. (2013) *Soft-Wired: How the New Science of Brain Plasticity Can Change Your Life*. San Francisco, CA: Parnassus Publishing. p. 233.

14 Merzenich, M. (2013) p. 233.

15 Desikachar, T. K. V. (1999) p. 51.

16 Nestor, J. (2020) *Breath: The New Science of a Lost Art*. New York: Riverhead Books.

17 Siviy, S. and Panksepp, J. (2011) In search of the neurobiological substrates for social playfulness in mammalian brains. *Neuroscience and Biobehavioral Reviews*, *35*(9), 1821–1830.

18 Huberman, A. (2020–21) Huberman Lab. www.hubermanlab.com. How Your Brain Works and Changes (1/1/20); Tools for Managing Stress and Anxiety (3/8/21).

19 Porges, S. (2021) p. 264; Porges, S. (2017) p. 82.

20 Hart Barnett, J. (2018) Three evidence-based strategies that support social skills and play among young children with autism spectrum disorders. *Early Childhood Education Journal, 46*(6), 665–672.

21 Maroso, M. (2023) A quest into the human brain. *Science, 382*, 166–167.

22 Siegel, D. (2012) *Pocket Guide to Interpersonal Neurobiology.* New York: W. W. Norton. p. 7-4.

23 Conrad, C. (2008) Chronic stress-induced hippocampal vulnerability: The glucocorticoid vulnerability hypothesis. *Reviews in the Neurosciences, 19*(6), 395–412.

24 Tollenaar, M. S. *et al.* (2008) The effects of cortisol increase on long-term memory retrieval during and after acute psychosocial stress. *Acta Psychologica, 127*(3), 542–552.

25 de Quervain, D. J. *et al.* (2000) Acute cortisone administration impairs retrieval of long-term declarative memory in humans. *Nature Neuroscience, 3*(4), 313–314.

Part II

1   Cohn, E. *et al.* (2000) Parental hope or therapy outcomes: Children with sensory modulation disorders. *American Journal of Occupational Therapy, 54*(1), 36–37.

2   Miller, L. J. (2006) p. 59.

Chapter 5

1   Prizant, B. (2015/2022) p. 57.

Chapter 6

1   Porges, S. (2017) p. 109.

2   Van der Kolk, B. (2015) *The Body Keeps the Score: Brain, Mind, and Body in the Healing of Trauma.* New York: Viking Press.

3   Levine, P. (2010) *In an Unspoken Voice: How the Body Releases Trauma and Restores Goodness.* Berkeley, CA: North Atlantic Press. p. 79.

4   Prizant, B. (2015/2022) pp. 21, 24.

Chapter 7

1   Emerson, D. and Hopper, E. (2011) *Overcoming Trauma through Yoga.* Berkeley, CA: North Atlantic Books. p. 121.

Chapter 9

1   Johnson, C. (1992). Coping and compassion fatigue. *Nursing, 22*(4), 116–121.

2   Figley, C. R. (1995). Compassion Fatigue: Toward a New Understanding of the Costs of Caring. In B. H. Stamm (ed.), *Secondary Traumatic Stress: Self-Care Issues for Clinicians, Researchers, and Educators* (pp. 3–28). Lutherville, MD: The Sidran Press.

3   Kornfield, J. (2008) *The Wise Heart.* New York: Bantam Books. Chapter 7.

4   Erickson, M. (1992) *Creative Choice in Hypnosis.* New York: Irvington Publishers. pp. 105, 216–217.

Chapter 11

1   Prizant, B. (2015/2022) p. 293.

Chapter 14

1   Stand behind a chair with the hands on the back. Releasing forward a very small distance (2 in/5 cm) sets everyone up for success. It's important for everyone (children and adults) to see the options.

PART VII

SUPPLEMENTAL RESOURCES

Support Materials to Copy, Download, Print, and Share

These resources are available to download, print, and share at www.greentreeyoga.org/differingneeds.

A. Art Project Samples: From templates and children's art

B. Shanti the Monkey

    1. Flip Chart: Shanti
    2. Shanti Coloring Sheets
    3. Activity Board Cards and Sample Chart

C. Art and Yoga Teaching Materials

    1. Three Practice Scripts (Chapter 10) (MP3s/PDF)
    2. Scripts (Chapter 14) (PDFs)
    3. Clipboard Notes
    4. MP3 Schedule
    5. Class Template
    6. Six Class Notes
    7. Planning Checklist
    8. Art Templates
    9. Feedback Form for Practice Scripts

D. Yoga Breaks for Children (MP3s/MP4s)

E. Self-Care Breaks (MP3s/MP4s/Handouts)

F. Getting Organized (Chapter 5: Preparations)

    1. Sample Flyers
    2. Parent Contacts and Follow-Up
        a. Activity Board Sample
        b. Coloring Sheets
        c. Follow-Up Questionnaire